The Game Fishes of New England and Southeastern Canada

The Game Fishes of New England and Southeastern Canada

Peter Thompson

Illustrated by Peter Thompson

Down East *Camden, Maine*

Order of Appearance

The Structure of Fishes

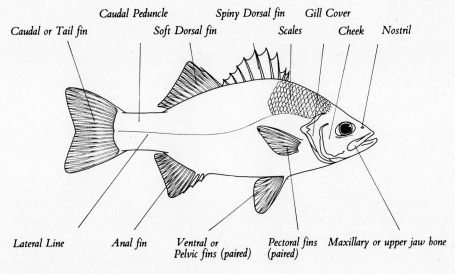

Caudal Peduncle

Caudal or Tail fin

Soft Dorsal fin

Spiny Dorsal fin

Gill Cover

Scales

Cheek

Nostril

Lateral Line

Anal fin

Ventral or
Pelvic fins (paired)

Pectoral fins
(paired)

Maxillary or upper jaw bone

External Anatomy / White Perch,
Morone americanus

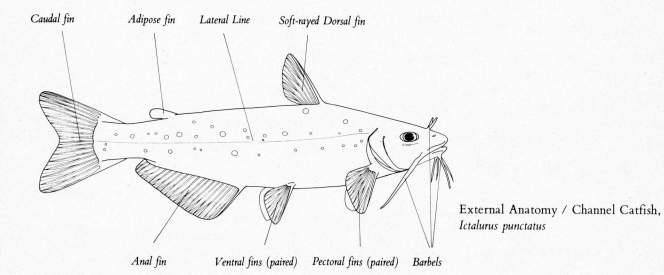

Caudal fin   Adipose fin   Lateral Line   Soft-rayed Dorsal fin

External Anatomy / Channel Catfish,
Ictalurus punctatus

Anal fin   Ventral fins (paired)   Pectoral fins (paired)   Barbels

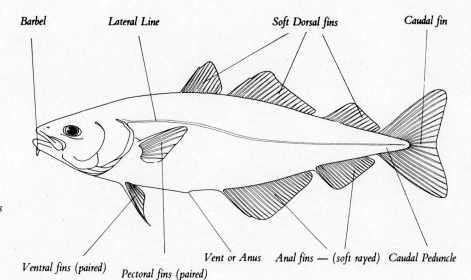

Barbel Lateral Line Soft Dorsal fins Caudal fin

External Anatomy / Pollock, *Pollachius virens*

Ventral fins (paired) Pectoral fins (paired) Vent or Anus Anal fins — (soft rayed) Caudal Peduncle

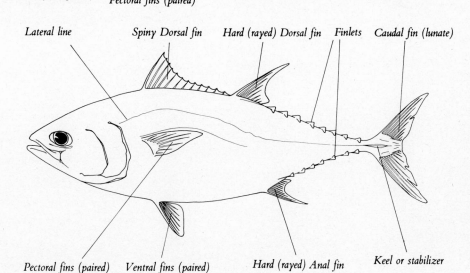

Lateral line Spiny Dorsal fin Hard (rayed) Dorsal fin Finlets Caudal fin (lunate)

External Anatomy / Bluefin Tuna, *Thunnus thynnus*

Pectoral fins (paired) Ventral fins (paired) Hard (rayed) Anal fin Keel or stabilizer

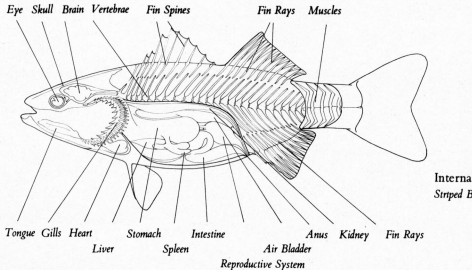

Eye Skull Brain Vertebrae Fin Spines   Fin Rays Muscles

Tongue Gills Heart   Stomach   Intestine   Anus Kidney Fin Rays
            Liver   Spleen   Air Bladder
                Reproductive System

Internal Anatomy of a typical bony fish /
Striped Bass, Morone saxatilis

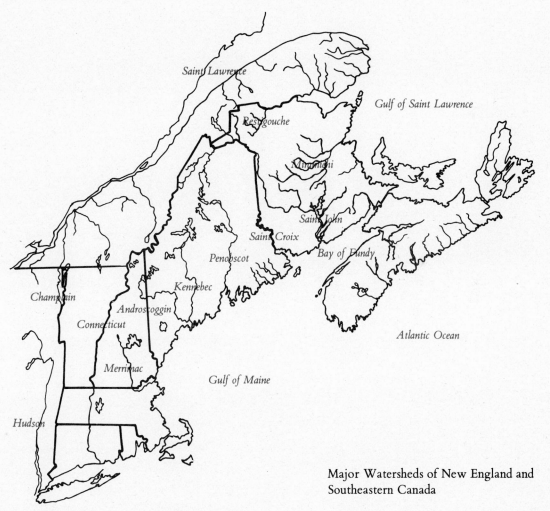

Saint Lawrence

Gulf of Saint Lawrence

Restigouche

Miramichi

Saint John

Saint Croix

Bay of Fundy

Penobscot

Champlain

Kennebec

Atlantic Ocean

Androscoggin

Connecticut

Merrimac

Gulf of Maine

Hudson

Major Watersheds of New England and
Southeastern Canada

1

Salt Water

Sharks

Blue Shark
Priorace glauca

Local Names:

- Great Blue Shark
- Blue Dog

Distinguishing Characteristics:

- Long, slender body
- Long, narrow pectoral fins
- Large, sharp teeth with serrated edges
- Dark blue color shading to lighter blue on flanks

Average Size:

- 10-14 feet (3-4 m.)
- 125-200 pounds (56-90 kg.)

Habits:

- A pelagic wanderer of the open sea
- Usually found far from shore
- Nearly always found near the surface, basking or in search of food

Like so many of the sharks found within our range, the blue shark is included here because it may occassionally be taken by anglers, especially in the more southerly areas. It may be encountered in regions where other sharks are commonly found, namely offshore or following warm surface water in search of prey.

Thresher Shark
Alopias vulpinus

Local Names:

- Thrasher
- Swiveltail
- Fox Shark

Distinguishing Characteristics:

- The oversized tail or caudal fin makes confusing this shark with other species impossible

6

- Sharp, smooth, rather weak teeth

Average Size:

- 12-16 feet (3-4 m.)
- 400-700 pounds (181-317 kg.)

Habits:

- Found close to shore in warm summer waters
- Usually but not always in shallow water
- Known to herd small forage fish with its large tail

Not commonly sought by anglers, the thresher is unique in the way it uses its enormous tail to herd bait fish. Often two fish will "work" together, driving their prey into a frenzy with their caudal fins. The sharks will then select and stun individual fish before devouring them.

The thresher's chief foods are mackerel, herring, menhaden, and bluefish. This distinctive fish gives a fast, strong fight when taken on rod and reel. Usually, heavy tackle and live or dead fish are used as bait.

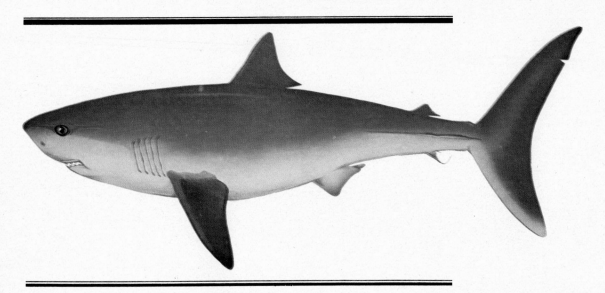

Great White
Shark

Carcharodon carcharias

Local Names:

- Man Eater, White Shark, White Pointer Shark, Blue Pointer Shark

Distinguishing Characteristics:

- Large size

8

- Large, triangular teeth
- Head has a blunt, rounded shape when seen from above

Average Size:

- 10-20 feet (3-6 m.)
- 1,000-1,500 pounds (450-680 kg.)

Habits:

- Found in offshore waters north to Newfoundland
- Pelagic, solitary or in small groups, usually remaining close to the surface in search of food
- Occasionally found near shore where it has been known to attack humans

Recently all sharks have been the object of much attention. The angling community has also joined the bandwagon. Because of its very nature, shark fishing will probably never enjoy the widespread popularity of trout or bass fishing, but there remains a small group of dedicated fishermen who like nothing better than to feel the strong rushes of a large shark at the end of their lines.

The great white shark, because of its enormous proportions, certainly would put any angler and even the best equipment to a severe test. These fish are usually found a good distance from shore, and large boats are required to reach the fishing grounds. Of course, heavy tackle and steel leaders are a must for any shark fishing. Baits can be almost any kind of animal flesh, alive or dead. When large sharks are located, it is often a simple matter to attract them to the hook. It is well-known that all sharks possess rather poor vision. For that reason, a bait that will produce an attractive scent (to the shark) is most commonly used.

All the larger sharks are much less than plentiful in our northern range (especially within the Gulf of Maine). In their northward migrations, they tend to follow the Gulf Stream. North of Cape Cod, Massachusetts, these fish are generally found too far at sea to be worth the average fisherman's attention.

Porbeagle Shark
Lamna nasus

Local Names:

- Mackerel Shark
- Blue Dog

Distinguishing Characteristics:

- Narrow, triangular teeth

11

- Similar to the great white shark, except that a more distinct color change occurs from dorsal to ventral
- Head and snout are pointed when seen from above

Average Size:

- 4-7 feet (1-2 m.)
- 75-150 pounds (33-70 kg.)

Habits:

- Open ocean
- Solitary or in small groups
- Found from the surface to great depths

This shark resembles the great white but is much smaller and less active. It is caught incidentally by anglers in our range. Since its habits are similar to those of the other larger sharks, it also does not attract much fishing pressure. When hooked, the porbeagle puts up a rather weak, sluggish battle. As with other sharks, a wide variety of baits will attract this fish.

Mako Shark
Isurus oxyrynchus

Local Names:

- Mackerel Shark
- Sharp-nosed Mackerel Shark
- Blue Pointer

Distinguishing Characteristics:

- Bluish-grev above, shading to dusky

13

- Long, thin teeth unevenly placed in jaw
- A very swift fish

Average Size:

- 6-12 feet (1-3 m.)
- 300-800 pounds (136-362 kg.)

Habits:
- Cosmopolitan in warm water, usually offshore
- Often found on or near the surface

The mako shark has long enjoyed a reputation as the most game of all the sharks. When hooked, this strong fish makes long, reel-jamming runs, and it has been known to leap from 20 to 30 feet (6-9 m.) into the air. It shares its voracious feeding habits with all of our other sharks; hence a cruising fish is relatively easy to hook once it has been found. As with the other sharks, the mako is common nowhere in our range.

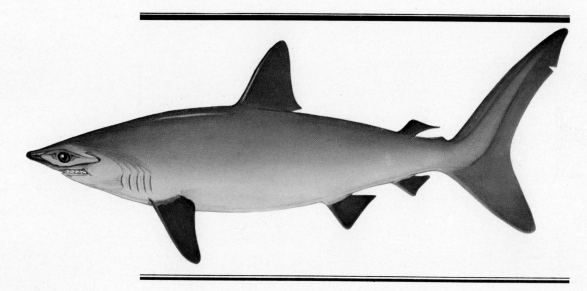

Hammerhead Shark

Sphyrna zygaena

Local Names:

- Shovelhead
- Shovelnose

Distinguishing Characteristics:

- The unusual shape of the head, with eyes set at the ends of long, flat protuberances (see detail)
- A heavy-bodied fish

15

Average Size:

- 10-12 feet (3-3.6 m.)
- 500-800 pounds (226-362 kg.)

Habits:

- A pelagic fish usually found swimming near the surface with the dorsal and upper caudal fins exposed
- Found in both inshore and offshore waters

Certainly unusual in appearance, the hammerhead is a typical shark in other respects. Usually found in the open ocean, it cruises alone or in small groups in search of smaller pelagic fishes for its food. Angling methods usually involve the use of heavy tournament-class equipment with trolled feather or fish baits or drifted live baits. On the saltwater flats in the Florida area, small hammerheads and their relative, the bonnet shark, are now sought by anglers using fly-fishing tackle. A powerful, pugnacious fish, the hammerhead will give even heavy tackle a real workout. The hammerhead, like our other sharks, is more a straggler than a regular visitor to our range. It is considered dangerous to man.

Dorsal View of Hammerhead Shark

Spiny Dogfish
Squalus acanthius

Local Names:

- Dogfish
- Piked Dogfish
- Grayfish

Distinguishing Characteristics:

- A small, slender shark
- Small, flattened teeth
- Both leading edges of dorsal fins have strong, sharp spines

18

Average Size:

- 2-4 feet (60-120 cm.)
- 5-10 pounds (2-4 kg.)

Habits:

- Found in deep and shallow water throughout our entire range
- Migrations are from offshore to inshore as the water warms and vice versa as it cools again in the fall
- Found from 20-30 feet (6-9 m.) down to the floor of the Continental Shelf

Any youngster who has spent a summer day fishing for cod, haddock, or flounder within our range has probably caught a spiny dogfish. They are sometimes known as "sand sharks," because they are often encountered in shallow water over sandy bottoms. They are naturally extremely voracious and will take any bait that reaches their level. In fact, at times when these fish are plentiful, it is often impossible for the fisherman to get his bait to the bottom where cod and haddock are found without first catching a dogfish. Dogfish are nearly always considered a nuisance. However, they do put up a strong, down-pulling, circling battle before they are brought to gaff. For this reason, they can provide a few hours (or days) of sport when other fish are not cooperating.

The spiny dogfish is by far the most common shark found in our region. It is, in fact, the only shark native to our waters.

Tunas, Bonitos, Mackerels

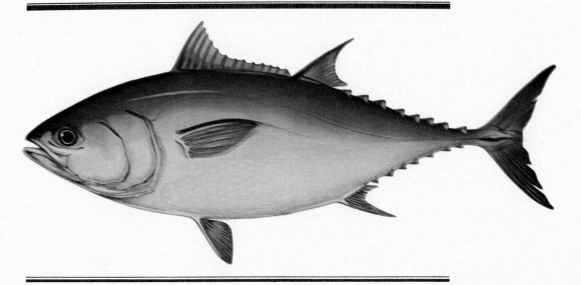

Bluefin Tuna
Thunnus thynnus

Local Names:

- Horse Mackerel
- Tuna
- Tunny

Distinguishing Characteristics:

- Large size
- The body is very deep and stout at the head, tapering rapidly to a very thin caudal peduncle

Average Size:

- 7-10 feet (2-3 m.)
- 350-800 pounds (158-362 kg.)

Habits:

- A migratory fish of the open sea
- Occasionally found quite close to shore
- Found in large schools, small groups, or as solitary individuals
- Feeds on smaller pelagic fishes and squid

The bluefin tuna is "the" big-game fish of the North Atlantic Ocean. There are few within our range that approach the massive proportions of this great fish. A long history and tradition has developed around this member of the mackerel family. A great deal has been written about the sport and commercial fishery based on this fish, and many clubs devoted to the pursuit of the bluefin have sprung up and disappeared along our Atlantic coast. Even now, the first fish of the summer will cause hundreds of fishermen to go

21

scrambling about rigging out boats to challenge the migrating schools of tuna.

As with their much smaller cousin, the Atlantic mackerel, the migratory pattern of the bluefin tuna appears to be generally east to west rather than north to south. This tuna is common throughout our range during every summer season. However, local populations in any area may fluctuate widely from year to year. Tuna are found in varying numbers throughout the Gulf of Maine and within the Bay of Fundy. However, Passamaquoddy Bay on the Maine-New Brunswick border is usually barren of this fish. Yet on several occasions bluefin tuna have been found in large numbers in that area as well. The yearly occurrence and abundance of these fish is extremely variable.

Recently the bluefin has come into its own as a food fish. To satisfy a growing Japanese market for these fish, many lobstermen have outfitted their boats with towers and "stands" in order to harpoon tuna during the summer months. Bluefin tuna has brought as much as $4.00 per pound at the docks in recent years. The fish are flown to Japan, where they are marketed fresh. The dark, oily flesh is considered a delicacy in that country. The canned tunafish so popular in American markets is usually the processed meat from albacore, a more southerly fish than the bluefin.

The remarkable bluefin tuna is taken by various methods. The most celebrated, of course, is the tournament-type rod and reel, using a sewn-on mackerel or squid, or a trolled "feather" lure with a bullet-shaped lead head as bait. But as the commercial market increases, more fishermen are turning to the harpoon as a more productive method of killing tuna. The harpooner's success depends largely upon perserverance and patience. However, the boat is certainly the single most important piece of equipment at his disposal. In the Gulf of Maine, and elsewhere, the traditional semi-open lobsterboat is the most commonly used craft. Towers, which may be as simple as a sturdy wooden pole with ladder-like steps and a seat on top, or as sophisticated as a modern radar tower, sprout high above the bridge of these tuna-chasers. The tower is used as a platform, where countless hours are spent scanning the sea for signs of tuna. To put the harpooner over the water and the fish, a stand is added to the bow of the boat. These stands, or "pulpits," consist of a couple of sturdy planks about 15 feet long, laid side by side and terminating in a kind of "crow's nest" affair to provide support for the harpooner.

The harpoon is made of a wooden shaft about 15 feet long and ending in a steel cowl, from which a sturdy metal rod protrudes. A triangular brass "dart" slips over the end of the rod. The dart is attached to a long length of nylon or polypropylene rope, which lies coiled on the forward deck when not in use. This rope is attached to one or more bamboo poles with large pieces of cork or foam attached to their lower portion. A flag completes the top part of this rig.

When the harpoon is thrown and strikes a fish, the dart penetrates the flesh and is held in place by several barbs. The harpoon shaft slips away from the dart and floats to the surface, and as the fish moves away, the line flows quickly into the water. The end of the line is attached to a buoy, which is thrown overboard and serves as a marker for the harpooned fish. The weight of all this gear eventually tires and kills the fish (often after several hours of swimming). Usually the "ironed" fish are allowed to swim away, trailing the flag, while others are sought. This is particularly true when several fish are encountered together. When the school sounds or no other fish are taken, the harpooned tuna are winched aboard the boat with a block and tackle, usually mounted at the top of a strong pole.

Recently, attempts have been made to regulate the taking of bluefin tuna. A one-fish-per-day limit has been set, and an extensive tagging program has been started. It is hoped that by regulating this fishery, we can prevent this great resource from being decimated.

Other methods used to take tuna are seining (usually schools of smaller fish are selected for this) and hand lining fish that have been attracted by a chum line.

Whatever method is used to take them, these remarkable fish provide a constant source of wonder and excitement for those who seek them.

False Albacore
Euthynnus alleteratus

Local Names:

- Little Tunny
- Bonito

Distinguishing Characteristics:

- More slender than the other small tunas
- Long, wavy, longitudinal bars on upper rear half of body

25

Average Size:

- 20-30 inches (50-76 cm.)
- 15-20 pounds (6-9 kg.)

Habits:

- Open water, offshore
- Schooling fish

Straggling around the elbow of Cape Cod, this active fish is found 5 to 20 miles from shore. It feeds largely on mackerel, herring, sand launce, squid, and other small fish. When plentiful, the false albacore provides sport equal to that of the other members of this group. Its excellent table qualities make it a prime quarry of sport and commercial fishermen.

Common Bonito

Sarda sarda

Local Names:

- Bonito
- Horse Mackerel

Distinguishing Characteristics:

- The body is entirely scaled as in other fish of this large family

27

- Has a large mouth ending at the rear margin of the eye
- Possesses large, strong teeth
- The first dorsal is long and straight in profile, unlike most other members of the mackerel clan found within our range
- Several dark bands on upper body

Average Size:

- 1½-2 feet (0.45-0.61 m.)
- 10-12 pounds (4-6 kg.)

Habits:

- Warm to warm-temperate seas
- Meanders in the Gulf Stream to the waters of Nova Scotia
- A fast-moving fish, usually found in large schools
- Feeds on mackerel, menhaden, alewives, squid, and sand launce

The common bonito is the only member of the bonito group that is more than a straggler to most of our region. It is taken as far north as Nova Scotia. However, only young specimens are taken in the more northerly parts of its range. The turning point for this fish might more realistically be assumed to be Cape Ann. This fish is usually found far from shore, and therefore only a relatively small number of fishermen have seen it.

In our range, the largest concentrations of this bonito are found south and west of Cape Cod. Here it may be taken by anglers fishing for other offshore species. It will take a wide variety of artificial and natural baits. This is a very strong, fast-swimming fish and affords excellent sport on light or medium tackle.

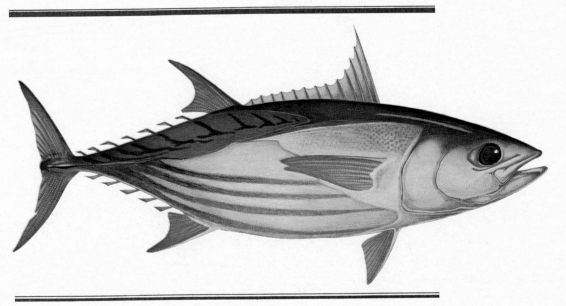

Skipjack Tuna

Euthynnus pelamis

Local Names:

- Oceanic Bonito
- Striped Bonito
- Skipjack

Distinguishing Characteristics:

- Stout body
- 4-6 dark longitudinal stripes below the lateral line
- Prominent corselet of scales on front third of body
- The first dorsal is high and steeply concave

Average Size:

- 1½-2 feet (0.45-0.61 m.)
- 5-15 pounds (2-6 kg.)

Habits:

- Found in warmer offshore waters
- Rarely found north or east beyond the elbow of Cape Cod
- A swift-moving, schooling fish

This attractive member of the mackerel family is another warm-water fish found only as a straggler north and east of Cape Cod. The skipjack tuna shares common characteristics with most of the other smaller tunas. Its speed, tendency to congregate in large schools, and fine flavor make this fish a favorite with sport and commercial fishermen around the world.

Atlantic Mackerel

Scomber scombrus

Local Names:

- Mackerel
- Tinker Mackerel

Distinguishing Characteristics:

- A very firm, cigar-shaped body
- All members of this family possess finlets dorsally and ventrally preceding the caudal fin

32

- An average of 27-30 dark vertical bars cover the upper third of the body

Average Size:

- 12-18 inches (30-45 cm.)
- 1-3 pounds (0.45-1 kg.)

Habits:

- A schooling fish, mackerel are often found in vast numbers
- Pelagic, swimming constantly in warm, oxygen-deficient water in order to maintain themselves
- Food is anything available in sufficient numbers, ranging from copepods and amphipods to shrimp, squid, and sand launce.

Anyone who has fished in the summer-warmed waters of our Atlantic Ocean has probably taken a mackerel. These fish are very common throughout our range. It is quite probable that the mackerel's migration is from deep to shallow water, rather than from south to north. Mackerel have been taken on the edge of the Continental Shelf during the winter months by commercial fishermen. When the water warms in the spring, vast shoals of these fish return to feed nearer the shore.

Mackerel serve a twofold purpose in the food chain. They prey on small copepods and amphipods, converting them to their own flesh. The mackerel then serves as forage for many species of larger fish, including striped bass, bluefish, and the tunas. In addition to this natural role, the mackerel has long been prized as a food fish. These oily fish are processed in many ways before reaching the world's tables. They are often available smoked, pickled, dried, or fresh.

For the sport fisherman, the prevalent mackerel serves as a readily accessible source of sport and fine eating. In their pursuit of food, mackerel often enter harbors, estuaries, and the surf along our beaches. When conditions are right and the mackerel are feeding, it is not uncommon to see anglers carrying 50 to 100 fish from their favorite spot. This fish is quite voracious and will strike any flashing silver spinner or live bait. In fact, when mackerel are in a "feeding frenzy," they will strike a bare hook while swarming only inches below the surface. To create these frenzies artificially, the experienced mackerel fisherman will use a chum slick, made up of cat food, oatmeal, ground sand launce, or ground parts of larger fish. The chum is bailed overboard and allowed to float off in a long line emanating from the boat. If there are mackerel in the area, they will soon show themselves and can be seen feeding on the chum. They come in such vast numbers that looking into the water, the fisherman may see these active fish stacked down to a depth of 20 to 30 feet. At this point a jig is worked rapidly among the feeding fish. One or more lures may be used, and taking a string of 4 to 5 mackerel on one line is not an unusual occurrence.

Light or ultra-light spinning or standard fly-fishing tackle is by far the most exciting method of taking these speedy fish.

Chub Mackerel

Scomber japonicus

Local Names:

- Hardhead Bullseye
- Bullseye

Distinguishing Characteristics:

- Very similar to Atlantic mackerel
- Eyes are considerably larger than those of the Atlantic mackerel

35

- Coloration below the lateral line consists of many dusky blotches, in contrast to the Atlantic mackerel, which is entirely silvery below the lateral line

Average Size:

- 8-14 inches (3-5 cm.)
- 1-2 pounds (0.45-0.91 kg.)

Habits:

- A pelagic surface schooling fish sharing the same habitat as the rest of the mackerel tribe
- Often found schooling with Atlantic mackerel

This fish is so similar to the more common Atlantic mackerel that nearly all pertinent information on the two species is interchangeable. However, it is interesting to note that the population of chub mackerel fluctuates much more widely than does that of its larger cousin. This fish has been known to disappear completely from the entire Atlantic coast for periods of twenty years or more. When populations do reappear, they increase to vast numbers in relatively short periods of time. Although many casual observers would not differentiate between the two species, there are some who prefer the table quality of the chub to the larger Atlantic mackerel. They do indeed provide equal sport.

36

Spanish Mackerels

Cero
Scomberomorus cavalla

Local Names:

- Cavalla
- Kingfish
- King Mackerel

Distinguishing Characteristics:

- Has no spots or other markings
- A very long, slender body

Average Size:

- 2-3 feet (0.61-0.91 m.)
- 10-20 pounds (4-9 kg.)

Habits:

- Favors open water, where it pursues smaller pelagic fishes for food
- South of our range it is often found quite close to shore
- Usually encountered in large schools
- An occasional straggler to southern New England

The cero and Spanish mackerel are the only members of this sub-group to enter our waters. They do so only as occasional stragglers that very seldom roam beyond Monomoy Point on the south shore of Cape Cod.

Similar in habits to our common mackerel, these fish are readily distinguished from the former by their strongly elongated body. It is unlikely that they would be mistaken for any fish other than Spanish mackerel types.

The cero and Spanish mackerel are included here because they might be taken occasionally by anglers in search of other pelagic species. In keeping with their family traits, these fish are fast and very game. In addition to its game qualities, the cero makes excellent table fare.

38

Spanish Mackerel

Scomberomorus maculatus

Local Names:

- Cero
- Spotted Mackerel

Distinguishing Characteristics:

- Dull, yellow-orange spots appear above and below the lateral line
- The first third of the first dorsal fin is black or grey
- The pectoral fins are scaled over about one half their length

39

Average Size:

- 18-24 inches (45-60 cm.)
- 2-5 pounds (0.91-2. kg.)

Habits:

- A cosmopolitan species, ranging widely through our warmer seas
- Usually found in large schools in search of smaller fishes
- A straggler to our northern waters

This fish is nearly identical to the closely related cero. It does however, range farther north than the former. It usually rounds the hook of Cape Cod each year, coming in greater numbers in particularly warm summers. Even for all that, the Spanish mackerel does not often leave the confines of Cape Cod Bay. The most northerly record of its appearance is at Monhegan Island.*

This attractive mackerel provides fine sport and equally good food.

*Bigelow & Schroeder, *Fishes of the Gulf of Maine*

Billfishes

Atlantic Sailfish
Istiophorus platypterus

Local Names:

- Sail
- Sailfish

Distinguishing Characteristics:

- A very large sail-like dorsal fin
- There may be more than one species of sailfish in the world's oceans, but their ranges do not overlap, so that the sail alone sets this fish apart from all other fishes in our region

Average Size:

- 6-8 feet (1-2 m.)
- 50-150 pounds (22-68 kg.)

Habits:

- Found in open water far from shore
- Usually encountered as solitary fish or in pairs; occasionally schooling

Wandering widely about the open ocean, the sailfish, like other billfishes, remains close to the surface. Sailfish are prized as game. Their flesh is of debatable quality, and very little is marketed. These very fast-swimming fish are at their sporting best when taken on light tackle. In fact, sailfish are rapidly gaining a following of fly-fishermen. Until recently, this fish was taken by trolling sewn-on skip-baits or artificial lures. But, if they can be sighted and approached, a fly caster can entice a fish to strike a skipping bug or popper. The sight of a sailfish cartwheeling or tail-walking at the end of a line is awesome indeed; the use of a fly rod only enhances this thrill.

This southern fish is included here because it is sometimes found following the warming effects of the Gulf Stream as it flows northward in the summer. It is nowhere plentiful in our waters, but occasional fish are taken nearly every year along the southern coast of New England.

White Marlin
Tetrapturus albidus

Distinguishing Characteristics:

- Short bill formed by elongation of upper jaws
- Frontal lobe of first dorsal is rounded
- A very slender, almost delicate fish

Average Size:

- 6-8 feet (1-2 m.)
- 50-150 pounds (22-68 kg.)

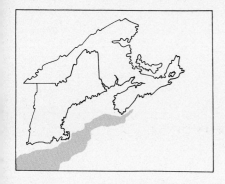

Habits:

- Open water, offshore
- Found near the surface
- Solitary or in schools

Of the four billfishes found within our range, the white marlin occurs farther north than any of the others. While still a fish of warm to warm-temperate seas, the white marlin has been taken off the coast of Nova Scotia.

This is one of the smallest billfishes and is distinguished in part by its "lightweight" appearance. But in spirit and action, the white marlin is the equal, on a pound-for-pound basis, of any of its closest relatives.

White marlin are found in relative abundance along the southern shores of our range, ending their northeastward movements (as a rule) at the elbow of Cape Cod. Those specimens taken in the Gulf of Maine and off Nova Scotia are very few in number and tend to be smaller than the average. In keeping with other members of this family, white marlin are encountered in schools, pairs, or as solitary fish. Their habits are identical to the other billfishes, in that they remain generally close to the surface in open water far offshore. They may be taken by trolling feather lures, strip baits, or whole, sewn-on fish. Favorite foods of this ocean wanderer are smaller schooling fishes and squids.

45

Blue Marlin
Makaira indica

Local Names:

- Cuban Black Marlin

Distinguishing Characteristics:

- Heavier overall than the closely related white marlin
- Light blue stripes on sides are much more pronounced than in the white marlin

46

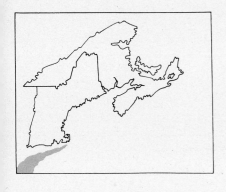

- Frontal lobe of first dorsal is pointed

Average Size:

- 7-9 feet (2.13-2.74 m.)
- 200-400 pounds (90-181 kg.)

Habits:

- Same as white marlin (*Tetrapturus albidus*)

The only major difference (other than anatomical) between this fish and the white marlin is that it is a much more southern fish. It is included here because it does straggle to the waters off Nantucket and Martha's Vineyard.

Everything pertinent to the white marlin applies to the blue.

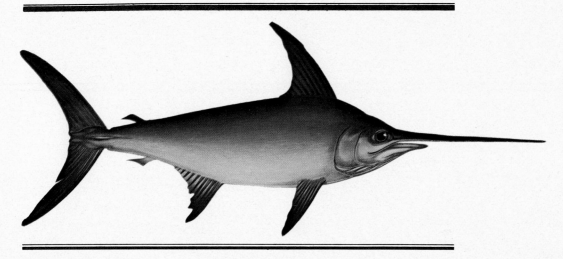

Swordfish
Xiphius gladius

Local Names:

- Broadbill

Distinguishing Characteristics:

- Large size
- Very long, heavy, flattened bill or sword up to one third of the fish's entire length
- Deep, stout body

48

Average Size:

- 8-12 feet (2.5-3.5 m.)
- 200-600 pounds (90-272 kg.)

Habits:

- Found inshore and offshore; often encountered in the haunts of the bluefin tuna
- Usually sighted as a single fish basking on the surface
- Feeds in deep water

A regular summer visitor to all our waters, the swordfish has a long-standing reputation as a superb gamefish and one of our most highly prized commercial fishes. Few restaurants on the Atlantic seaboard do not include swordfish on their menus, and for good reason — the flesh of this great fish is firm and mild flavored.

Even when plentiful, swordfish do not school. Their lack of the desire for company means that not more than two fish are sighted together. They are most often found lying nearly motionless or cruising lazily on the surface. In traveling in this fashion, these large fish can be easily distinguished by the high, pointed dorsal and trailing caudal fin, the latter usually only partly exposed. Sighting a swordfish in this attitude allows a harpooner an easy kill. When on the surface, these fish seem without fear and can be approached so that the stand or pulpit carrying the harpooner is directly above the fish.

Wherever big-game fishermen put to sea, an encounter with a

swordfish is gladly accepted. Ernest Hemingway in his unfinished novel, *Islands in the Stream*, has provided us an intense portrait of just such an encounter with a giant broadbill.

The method most often used in angling for these powerful fish is trolling from a medium-sized boat, such as the type used for tuna or marlin fishing. The tackle consists of large-capacity tournament-type reels and short, stiff, trolling rods with roller guides to reduce line friction. The baits are usually whole mackerel or squid sewn onto the large hook in a manner that allows them to bounce about on the water while trolled at a moderate speed. Generally, two rigs are set, one on either side of the boat. The lines are held outside the boat's wake by outriggers to which they are attached by a clothespin. The outriggers are long poles set at about a 45-degree angle and suspended over the water from a point somewhere amidship.

As the boat moves forward, the baits skip across the surface of the water. When a fish takes one of the baits, the pressure pulls the line from the clothespin. That tell-tale "snap" is the signal for the angler to take the rod and position himself in the fighting chair in the stern of the boat. Angler, crew, and boat then become a team, all working to boat a fish usually outweighing the fisherman by several hundreds of pounds. The skipper drives the boat in forward or reverse to gain line or a better position from which to play the fish. The mate acts as coach and tends to the straining angler's needs by maneuvering the fighting chair or mopping the angler's brow. Many of these battles have taken whole days and still ended in a parted line and a weary fisherman with blistered hands, sunburned face and arms, and what he or she might well refer to as a "broken back".

Jacks, Dolphins, Bluefish

Crevalle Jack
Caranx hippos

Local Names:

- Jack

Distinguishing Characteristics:

- Body is compressed laterally
- Bony scutes covering lateral line on rear third of body
- Steeply rounded, high forehead

Average Size:

- 1-3 feet (0.30-0.91 m.)
- 2-20 pounds (0.91-9 kg.)

Habits:

- An inshore fish frequenting bays and reefs

The crevalle jack is generally a southern fish common in the Florida area. Like so many other fishes found in warm-temperate seas, this jack follows the Gulf Stream northward in summer months. Hence, it is a regular visitor to the area around Woods Hole, Massachusetts.

These are pelagic, schooling fish that behave in much the same manner as does our common Atlantic mackerel. When driving and feeding on bait fishes, a school of these predators can cause enough commotion to make themselves heard as much as one-half mile away. Their speed and voracious appetite make them a favorite sport fish wherever they are common.

Included here because it is a regular, if scarce, visitor to our range, the crevalle jack can be found as far north and east as the southern shores of Cape Cod. A specimen may sometimes be taken by anglers fishing for mackerel or bluefish.

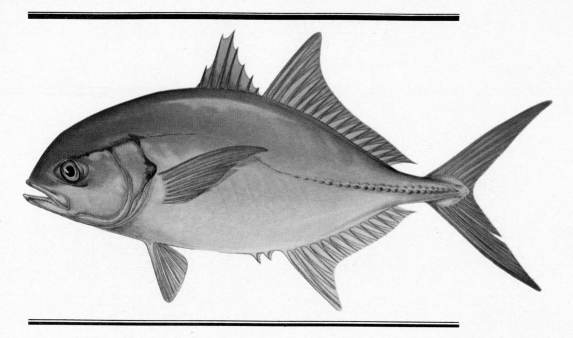

Hardtail

Caranx crysos

Local Names:

- Yellow Jack
- Runner
- Yellow Mackerel

54

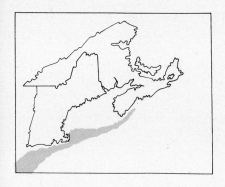

Distinguishing Characteristics:

- Bony scutes along rear half of lateral line
- Much thinner in profile than the crevalle jack, yet still relatively high and compressed

Average Size:

- 12-24 inches (30-61 cm.)
- 1-6 pounds (0.45-2.72 kg.)

Habits:

- Inshore and around reefs or ledges
- A schooling fish

This is the most common member of the jack tribe to be found in our northern waters. It is a fairly frequent visitor to Nova Scotian waters, but the records from these northern outposts are all of relatively small specimens. Its habits are very similar to those of the crevalle jack. Where this fish is common, it has become a favorite of fly-fishermen. It shares its larger cousin's game qualities and is reputed to far outdistance the larger jack in terms of flavor.

Dolphin
Coryphaena hippurus

Local Names:

- Dorado

Distinguishing Characteristics:

- Only one other fish, the pompano dolphin, *C. equisetis*, which does not enter our waters, is similar to the dolphin

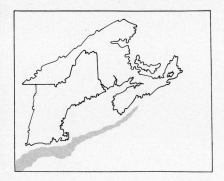

- Males have a very high forehead, which is quite square in profile
- Females have a much more gradually sloping forehead
- Both sexes possess a single, long, spineless dorsal fin

Average Size:

- 3-6 feet (0.91-2.0 m.)
- 10-15 pounds (4-22 kg.)

Habits:

- An extremely swift fish of the open water
- Usually found far from shore in waters shared with the tunas, bonitos, and billfishes
- Encountered singly or in schools

This brilliantly colored pelagic wanderer is an occasional visitor to our southern New England coasts. Usually found far from shore, the dolphin has been known to straggle north and east to the waters of Nova Scotia. By remaining offshore and close to the Gulf Stream, it has nearly always avoided the Gulf of Maine, with its colder average temperatures. Nowhere within our range is the dolphin a common species. Its largest northeastern concentration is off the islands of Nantucket and Martha's Vineyard.

This extremely fast-swimming fish has developed a reputation as an unsurpassed sport fish. It takes a wide variety of fish baits and artificials. As

57

more fly-rodders go down to the salt, this remarkable fish is being increasingly sought by users of the long rod. When hooked, the vibrant dolphin puts on a spectacular show, which includes long, fast surface runs and high, twisting jumps. When this fish is killed, its rainbow colors rapidly fade to a dull, uniform hue. The dolphin maintains a reputation as prime table fare.

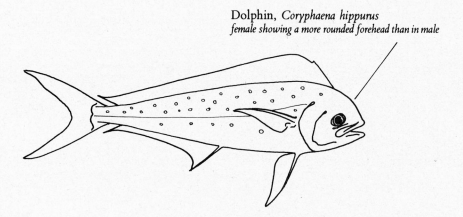

Dolphin, *Coryphaena hippurus*
female showing a more rounded forehead than in male

Bluefish

Pomatomus saltatrix

Local Names:

- Blue
- Snapper (young fish)
- Tailor

Distinguishing Characteristics:

- Large mouth filled with many strong, sharp teeth
- Bears some anatomical resemblance to the jacks to which it is most closely related

59

- A long, well-developed spineless second dorsal preceded closely by a much smaller first dorsal having 7 or 8 stout spines
- Slightly projecting lower jaw
- Deeply forked caudal fin

Average Size:

- 18-30 inches (45-76 cm.)
- 2-10 pounds (0.91-4 kg.)

Habits:

- Usually found in large schools
- A pelagic wanderer, following bait fishes such as mackerel, menhaden, and other schooling fishes
- A voracious predator with a seemingly insatiable appetite
- Found in tidal rivers, estuaries, along beaches and rocky shores, and in the open sea

The bluefish has a reputation as one of the most voracious fish living in salt water. When schools of these swift, schooling predators are feeding, they will strike almost anything that moves. Bathers who happen to be among a school of bluefish have often been bitten by these fish. When pursued by bluefish, their prey will occasionally beach themselves in an attempt to elude the larger fish.

Because of their feeding and schooling habits, bluefish are ideal sport fish. They are also among the tastiest fish found in our waters. Anglers who encounter schools of bluefish will find them willing to savagely devour lures or baits presented with any kind of fishing tackle. Live bait, surface or swimming plugs, spinning lures and jigs, streamer flies, and fly-rod poppers will all produce violent strikes when feeding bluefish are located. When these fish are known to be in an area but are not "showing," chumming is often an effective method for attracting them.

The migrations of these fine fish have remained something of a mystery. They appear to congregate only where and when large schools of bait are available. Yet they have been known to disappear from an area for many years, even when mackerel, herring, or menhaden are abundant. Such has been the case in the Gulf of Maine as far south as northern Massachusetts. During the past several years, bluefish have returned to Maine and New Hampshire waters (in varying numbers) after an absence of about 25 years. During the entire period of their absence, mackerel and herring were encountered in average to above-average numbers. When the bluefish did return (in vast schools) their presence caused understandable excitement. Many anglers were hospitalized with wounds inflicted to a careless hand, finger, or foot by a recently boated bluefish.

Bluefish have remained common in our range all along the southern shores and as far north as Cape Ann, Massachusetts, and as a frequent stray in Nova Scotian waters. Unlike the mackerel and some other common saltwater species, the migratory patterns of this fish seem to be from north to south. In the winter months, bluefish are very common in Florida waters, returning to their northern ranges in May, June, or July, depending upon the area.

The Sea Basses

Striped Bass
Morone saxatilis

Local Names:

- Rock
- Linesides
- Bass
- Striper
- Rock Bass

62

Distinguishing Characteristics:

- Greenish or bronze back with silver flanks distinctly marked by dark, horizontal lines
- Large size

Average Size:

- 18-30 inches (45-76 cm.)
- 2-20 pounds (0.91-9 kg.)

Habits:

- Found in coastal waters north to the Gulf of St. Lawrence
- Cruises the surf in search of forage fish
- Ascends rivers south of our range to spawn in fresh water and can be be found in great numbers in the brackish water of marine estuaries

For the majority of coastal sport fishermen in New England and southeastern Canada, the striped bass is "the" game fish. The large size, excellent fighting qualities, and delectable flavor of this remarkable fish justify all the excitement and frustration that it causes.

Seasoned surfmen who cruise the beaches year after year still have reason to wonder about the unpredictable behavior of the striped bass. No matter how long a fisherman pursues this great fish, he will always have his fair share of fishless days when nothing will produce action.

The striped bass will take a very wide variety of lures and baits. In recent years there has been a great increase in the use of the fly rod in striped bass fishing. Popping bugs skipped along the surface and large streamers tied on stainless-steel hooks are responsible for taking growing numbers of fish each season. In heavy surf or deep tidal rips, a surf spinning or casting outfit is a necessity. Rods for this type of angling range from nine to twelve feet and are fitted with reels having large line capacities. Surface or deep-running plugs are often nine or ten inches long. Live bait is a long-time favorite with deepwater bass fishermen. Live eels carefully rigged and drifted on a running tide account for some of the largest striped bass taken each year. Live mackerel, herring, or menhaden are also favorite baits.

From Cape Cod and the outer islands to Newburyport, Massachusetts, one can find some of the world's best striped bass fishing. Each spring and fall, the Cape Cod Canal, Martha's Vineyard, and the beaches around Race Point in Provincetown see crowds of hopeful casters working the surf. During these periods of migration, very large fish called "bulls" or "cows" can be found very close to shore. These larger bass will mingle with "school bass" averaging 5 to 12 pounds. Encountering a feeding school of these strong fish will leave the fisherman with weary arms and a happy smile.

A casual look at the striped bass fishery on the Atlantic coast would suggest that all is well. However, during the spawning season of 1976, large numbers of mature bass were exposed to chemicals known as PCBs. This insidious material was discharged from factories in the Chesapeake Bay area. This large fertile estuary produces an estimated 60 percent of all the striped bass found on the Atlantic seaboard. The result of this exposure has not yet been documented, but it is known that PCBs will cause sterility in sexually mature fish. We can only hope that the future of the striped bass does not hold their inclusion on the "endangered species" list.

64

Sea Bass
Centropristes striatus

Local Names:

- Black Sea Bass
- Blackfish

Distinguishing Characteristics:

- All fins are quite large in relation to the body
- The first and second dorsals form one continuous fin

- The upper lobe of the caudal fin terminates in a thread-like projection

Average Size:

- 12-24 inches (30-60 cm.)
- 1-3 pounds (0.45-1 kg.)

Habits:

- Can be found inshore and offshore
- Usually encountered in small groups around rocks or other protrusions over hard bottoms

The sea bass is limited to a rather short range, from Virginia northward as far as the south shore of Cape Cod. Rarely does one of these fish enter the Gulf of Maine, and there are no records of sea bass in Canadian waters.

This fish is generally found on or near the bottom of the sea. In summer it is often found in shallow water close to shore. The winter months find sea bass in 30 to 70 fathoms of water generally far from shore. When they are found within easy reach of the sport fisherman, sea bass are very willing to take the hook. Baits similar to those used for other ground fish, such as clams, worms, crabs, or fish, will serve quite well to take sea bass. They are strong fish and put up a good battle when taken on light tackle. Like its cousin, the striped bass, the sea bass has fine, white flesh with an excellent flavor.

White Perch
Morone americana

Local Names:

- Silver Perch
- Sea Perch

Distinguishing Characteristics:

- Resembles the striped bass in shape, and number and placement of fins

- Differs from *M. saxatilis* in having a much smaller head and mouth
- There is no space between the two dorsal fins

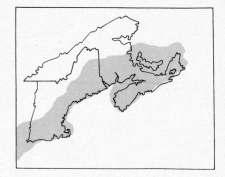

Average Size:

- 8-12 inches (20-30 cm.)
- 8-16 ounces (226-453 g.)

Habits:

- Coastal population is anadromous, spawning in April, May, and June within our region
- Generally found close to shore in shallow water, especially in estuaries and saltwater "ponds"
- There are many landlocked populations scattered throughout our range
- Since this is a very prolific fish, landlocked populations tend to become over-crowded, resulting in large numbers of small, growth-stunted fish

Even the coastal populations of this fish do not enter very deep water. They are found primarily in estuaries and bays close to shore.

The white perch is one of our cleanest game fish in terms of table quality. It is subject to no internal parasites, so it remains an attractive food fish regardless of water temperature. As a game fish, this small member of the sea bass group provides excellent sport on light spinning or fly tackle. It is extremely voracious and willing to take any lure or bait that comes within reach. Its willingness to oblige sportsmen, its fine, sweet flavor, and the large numbers found in accessible waters combine to make the white perch a favorite of young and old anglers alike. It is, in fact, considered a pest in many areas where very large numbers of these fish have taken over habitat suited for other game fish.

When white perch are entering their native streams to spawn in the spring of the year, crowds of fishermen will stand elbow-to-elbow in order to take home pails of these fish for a fishfry or for the freezer. At other times of the year, anglers will usually troll slowly through their favorite waters in search of white perch. When one fish is taken, usually the boat is stopped and the sport begins, because where there is one white perch, there are usually many more.

During the warmer months, schools of white perch can often be found near the surface late in the afternoon or early evening. At these times the angler equipped with a light fly rod can enjoy hours of fine sport as these scrappy fighters seem to line up to take a streamer or wet fly.

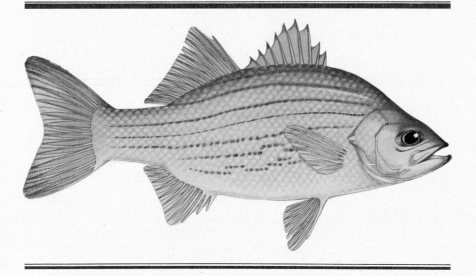

White Bass
Morone chrysops

Local Names:

- Silver Bass
- White Lake Bass
- Bar Blanc

Distinguishing Characteristics:

- Deep bodied and laterally compressed
- Small, sharp teeth

70

- Slightly projecting lower jaw

Average Size:

- 10-12 inches (25-30 cm.)
- ¾-1½ pounds (0.33-0.67 kg.)

Habits:

- Travels in large schools, often near the surface
- Usually occurs in lakes and larger rivers

The white bass is very similar to the white perch in its habits, except that it does not run to sea as does the perch.

M. chrysops supports a small commercial fishery in the Great Lakes region, but it is usually considered a game fish. It is most available to anglers in the spring of the year, as it moves inshore and into rivers and streams to spawn. At this time great numbers of this fish are taken by fishermen using spinning tackle or fly rods and streamer flies. It shares with the white perch its firm, white flesh of excellent flavor (especially when taken from clear, cold water.)

Wrasses

Cunner
Tautogolabrus adspersus

Local Names:

- Perch
- Sea Perch
- Achigan de Mer
- Tanche

72

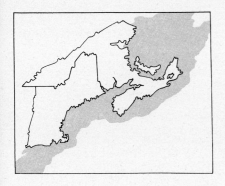

Distinguishing Characteristics:

- Stout body and caudal peduncle
- Rounded fins
- Dorsal fins form one continuous whole, with no demarkation between first and second other than the spine of the former
- Extremely variable in color
- Strong jaws with short, blunt teeth used for crushing mollusks

Average Size:

- 6-12 inches (15-30 cm.)
- 8-16 ounces (226-453 g.)

Habits:

- A bottom dweller, usually remaining close to shore
- Generally congregates around weed-covered reefs, around wharves and pilings, and in shallow, rocky coves
- Usually encountered in loose schools, which appear to scatter over a fairly wide area
- Usually found in great numbers

The cunner is a curious and very interesting fish. Usually considered a pest by sports fishermen in search of larger species, the cunner maintains a secure position in the intertidal zone. A member of the wrasse family, the cunner is found in widely varying concentrations throughout our range and northward as well. For largely unstudied reasons, this fish will appear in great numbers and disappear almost completely some years later from any locality. However, when the cunner is present, it's nearly always found in vast numbers.

Catching one of these greedy fish is a very simple matter. Nearly any rocky cove will serve as a home for this fish, and all the angler need do is bait a hook with clam, sea worm, mussel, or artificial lure, toss the rig into the surf and wait — usually only a few minutes. As soon as the fish become aware of the bait, they will swarm around the area and any number of them can be caught.

Tautog

Tautoga onitis

Local Names:

- Blackfish

Distinguishing Characteristics:

- Steep, high, rounded forehead
- The first or spined dorsal is noticeably higher than the second

- Very stout body
- Very high, thick, caudal peduncle
- All fins are rounded in profile

Average Size:

- 18-30 inches (45-76 cm.)
- 2-6 pounds (0.91-2. kg.)

Habits:

- Remains even closer to shore than does the cunner
- Habitat preference is very similar to that of the cunner — around rocky reefs, wharves, pilings, and the like
- Feeds chiefly on mollusks, which, like the cunner, it crushes with its stout, blunt teeth

Like the cunner, the tautog is a member of the wrasse family. Its range is predominantly to the south of the cunner's. It is quite common on the shores of Connecticut, Rhode Island, and the south shore of Cape Cod, Massachusetts. However, this fish does occur in Canadian waters as far north and east as Halifax, Nova Scotia. As with the more numerous cunner, the tautog has been known to disappear for varying periods only to reappear at some later date.

The tautog is usually found in very shoal water and quite close to shore. Bigelow and Schroeder in *Fishes of the Gulf of Maine* state that "it is unusual to catch one, more than 3 to 4 miles from shore or 30 to 60 feet deep." Sharing the cunner's preference for reefs and rocks, this larger fish is a good source of sport for the light-tackle angler. In fact, in recent years a rather extensive sport fishery has developed around this fish in the waters surrounding Yarmouth, Nova Scotia.

The tautog will take a wide variety of natural baits, showing a preference for sea worms. Being gregarious and generally quite abundant, this fish is often sought by youngsters to provide hours of fishing fun. Like the cunner, however, they are rather bony, but the flesh is sweet tasting and (some feel) worth the effort.

Porgies

Local Names:

- Porgy

78

Scup

Stenotomus chrysops

Distinguishing Characteristics:

- A deep, laterally compressed body
- Forehead is slightly depressed in the vicinity of the eye
- The entire dorsal fin can be flattened into a groove running along the back
- Long, pointed pectorals
- Deeply lunate, large caudal fin

Average Size:

- 12-16 inches (30-40 cm.)
- 1-3 pounds (0.45-1 kg.)

Habits:

- An inshore fish in warm weather, moving offshore to deeper water in winter
- Usually encountered in schools
- A bottom feeder, favoring hard, smooth, or rocky areas
- The general range of the scup is from the south shore of Cape Cod south to the Virginia coast
- This fish apparently follows an irregular north-south migration pattern

The scup, being similar to the cunner and tautog in feeding and habitat preference, provides a great deal of sport to anglers working inshore waters with live bait. Its schooling habits combined with a voracious appetite make this a rather easy mark for the light tackle enthusiast. Sea worms, clams, and cut fish baits account for the lion's share of the catch.

Where this fish is plentiful, it is actively sought by commercial fishermen. Because of its preference for shoal waters close to shore, the most practical method for taking this fish in marketable numbers is by the use of fish traps and pound nets. The flavor and texture of this fish when cooked is considered among the best. This fact adds a bonus for the sport fisherman in search of food and game.

Sheepshead
Archosargus probatocephalus

Distinguishing Characteristics:

- Very high, steep forehead having a straight-line profile
- Stout, blunt teeth and jaws
- Very deep, laterally compressed body
- Six to eight dark vertical bars on the sides

81

Average Size:

- 18-30 inches (46-76 cm.)
- 4-20 pounds (2-9 kg.)

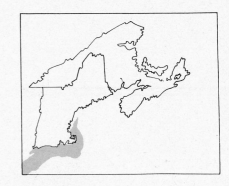

Habits:

- Inshore, on or near the bottom
- Found around rocky reefs, shoals, and wharves
- Feeds chiefly on mollusks, including clams, mussels, and squid when available

Sheepshead, with their black and white vertical stripes and clown-like appearance, are very attractive to the inshore saltwater angler not only for their sporting qualities but also for their fine flavor.

Unfortunately for those of us living in New England and the Canadian Maritimes, this fish's range is quite restricted to the coasts of the south and central United States. Sharing all other habits with the more northerly scup, the sheepshead provides good sport and fine eating.

Only a very few of these fish ever round the elbow of Cape Cod. A few have been reported in St. John Harbor in New Brunswick, but these reports were never very well substantiated. In fact, during the past 30 years, the sheepshead's range appears to have been shrinking southward, with its northward wanderings ending generally around New York.

Croakers & Kin

Weakfish

Cynoscion regalis

Local Names:

- Sea Trout
- Grey Sea Trout
- Squeteague
- Squit

Distinguishing Characteristics:

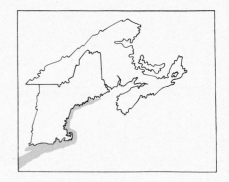

- Body elongated
- Large mouth, bearing small, strong teeth; lower jaw protrudes slightly beyond upper
- Long second dorsal of even height, preceded by a rather pointed, spiny first dorsal
- Body is sprinkled with small, dark spots resembling the freshwater trouts, hence its common name

Average Size:

- 18-30 inches (46-76 cm.)
- 2-8 pounds (0.91-4 kg.)

Habits:

- A schooling fish
- Usually found in estuaries and salt flats often where eel grass is present
- Feeds on squid, shrimp, herring, and other locally abundant forage fish

The weakfish is another fish whose range is concentrated south of New England and appears north of Cape Cod primarily as a stray. However, for a

84

few relatively short periods (separated by long absences), the weakfish has been quite common within the confines of Massachusetts Bay. It has been known to stray as far north as the Bay of Fundy.

Where it is abundant, the weakfish maintains a very devoted following of enthusiastic sport fishermen. It will take a wide variety of baits and artificial lures. Fly-rod anglers will find this excellent game fish willing to take a surface popper worked over the grassy areas of shallow bays and estuaries. When hooked this fish must be treated with great care — the name weakfish derives from the fact that the flesh around its mouth is quite soft and easily torn. Encountering a feeding school of these fish in a sheltered bay can provide the seasoned light-tackle angler with fine sport and an equally fine meal.

Whiting

Menticirrhus saxatilis

Local Names:

- Kingfish
- King Whiting
- Minkfish

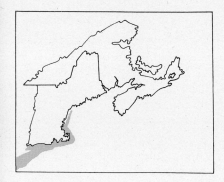

Distinguishing Characteristics:

- The placement of fins and body shape are similar to the weakfish
- Short chin barbel
- A high, pointed first dorsal fin (with third spine projecting much higher than the rest) is followed by a long, low, second dorsal
- The snout overhangs the lower jaw
- Lower caudal lobe is rounded (in profile), while upper is slightly pointed

Average Size:

- 12-17 inches (30-43 cm.)
- ½-3 pounds (0.22-1 kg.)

Habits:

- An inshore fish preferring hard or sandy ground
- A bottom feeder that usually occurs in schools
- Feeds primarily on shrimp and (somewhat less frequently) on crabs, worms, and small fishes

The usual range of this fine fish is from Chesapeake Bay to New York. It is a regular (although uncommon) summer visitor to the southern extremities of our range. It has been recorded as far north as Casco Bay, Maine, but only as a stray.

Unlike most bottom dwellers, the whiting provides fine sport. Where it is common, it is often taken from the surf. It is a rather small fish with very tasty flesh, much of which finds its way to the commercial markets in the mid-Atlantic states.

Freshwater Drum

Aplodinotus grunniens

Local Names:

- Gray Bass
- Sheepshead
- White Perch

- Grunter
- Gaspergore
- Malachigan

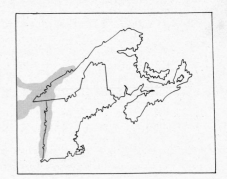

Distinguishing Characteristics:

- A laterally compressed body with a high, sloping forehead
- Mouth (of moderate size) has thin upper jaw terminating at about the mid-point of the eye
- Snout overhangs mouth
- Ventral fins have a short, treadlike extension on their leading edges

Average Size:

- 18-20 inches (46-51 cm.)
- 1-5 pounds (0.45-2 kg.)

Habits:

- Usually found in large, clear, shallow lakes, ponds, and rivers
- A bottom feeder that preys mainly on mollusks and worms

The freshwater drum is the only member of its family that spends its entire life in fresh water. Reports on its quality as food and game vary widely,

90

depending upon which fisherman does the reporting. It is most often sought by commercial fishermen, but will provide good sport when taken on light tackle.

This drum is a bottom feeder and will strike a wide variety of natural baits, and occasionally take an artificial lure. It is usually caught by anglers fishing for other species. Its fight is so strong and active that it is sometimes confused with the smallmouth bass.

The flesh of this fish is white and takes the form of large, coarse flakes. The commercial catch is most often used as food for mink being raised by fur ranchers in the Great Lakes region.

"Ground" Fishes

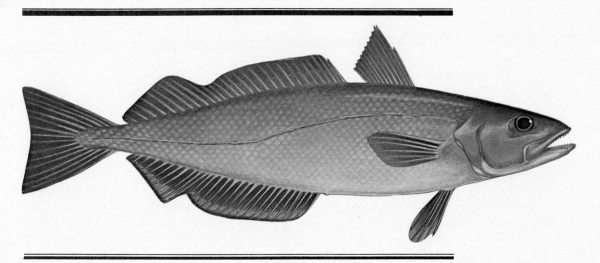

Silver Hake

Merluccius bilinearis

Local Names:

- Whiting
- New England Hake

Distinguishing Characteristics:

- Two separate, soft-rayed dorsal fins, with the second much longer than the first
- Has no chin barbel as do the true hakes
- A slender fish, with large eyes and mouth
- Has two or more rows of sharp teeth
- The lower jaw projects slightly beyond the upper

Average Size:

- 12-30 inches (31-76 cm.)
- 1-5 pounds (0.45-2 kg.)

Habits:

- A voracious predator feeding on any forage available, including mackerel, herring, alewives, butterfish, silversides, and squid when available
- May be taken close to shore or far from it, in shallow or deep water
- Congregates in large numbers into loose groups

The silver hake is a very interesting fish in that its habits are quite diverse. At times this fish will behave as a bottom fish (having been taken from 400 fathoms of water). At other times, silver hake can be found feeding so close to shore and in such shallow water that they will beach themselves in pursuit of

93

their prey. This fish is common throughout our range, inshore in summer, and in deeper water offshore in the colder months. Their breeding range is primarily within Gulf of Maine waters. Eggs identified as from silver hake have been collected off the Nova Scotian coast around Halifax. The southern limit for this fish is around the region of New York and New Jersey.

Forming an important part of the commercial catch in our waters, the silver hake is also sought by sport fishermen, usually in the surf along beaches. Feeding primarily at night, hake are often taken by anglers fishing for striped bass and flounder.

As its habits indicate, the silver hake will take a very wide variety of baits and artificial lures. Sea worms, clams, cut or whole fish, and many types of jigs and metal squids will all take this fine table fish. The flesh is very sweet tasting but will soon soften if not consumed when quite fresh. For that reason it was not until the early twentieth century that many of these fish were sold commercially. But, with the advent of satisfactory freezing methods, silver hake has become a mainstay in the commercial fisherman's catch, ranking very high on comparative market ratings.

White Hake

Merluccius merluccius

Local Names:

- Boston Hake
- Hake
- Black Hake
- Mud Hake
- Ling
- Merluche
- Lingue

Distinguishing Characteristics:

- First of two dorsal fins is sharply triangular, tapering to a thin filament that is generally longer than the fin proper
- Second dorsal is quite long, beginning at the rear edge of the first and continuing to the caudal peduncle. It is much lower than the first dorsal
- Ventral fins form a thin, forked filament extending to the leading edge of the anal fin
- Head and mouth are large with maxillary extending to the rear margin of the eye

Average Size:

- 24-36 inches (61-91 cm.)
- 5-10 pounds (3-5 kg.)

Habits:

- Young fish (fry) are commonly found at the water's surface, close to shore
- Mature fish are bottom dwellers but may be taken at almost any depth
- Can withstand a very wide range of temperatures
- Prefers mud or soft bottom

The white hake is a weak swimmer and is not very game when hooked. It feeds primarily at night and is often taken by anglers fishing for striped bass after dark. Hake feed chiefly on shrimps, amphipods, and small crustaceans. They are also fond of squid and small fishes.

This fish is not commonly sought by anglers, but will take a wide variety of natural baits. It is a good food fish although its flesh is not so firm as haddock. However, the hakes comprise a fair percentage of the commercial catch.

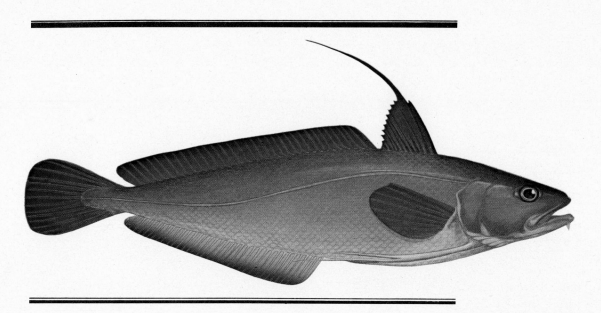

Squirrel Hake
Urophycis chuss

Local Names:

- Red Hake
- Ling

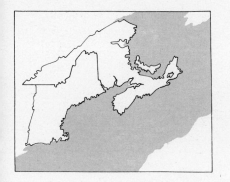

Distinguishing Characteristics:

- Nearly identical to the white hake
- Mouth is not as large as in the white. The upper jaw extends only to the mid-point of the eye
- The ventral fin (or filament) is longer than in the white hake, extending slightly beyond the leading edge of the anal fin
- Pectoral fin is larger and more rounded than in the white hake
- Slightly larger scales than in the white

Average Size:

- 18-24 inches (46-61 cm.)
- 2-6 pounds (1-3 kg.)

Habits:

- Identical to those of the white hake

The squirrel hake is so nearly identical to the white that only close inspection will differentiate the two. They share the same habitat and are ranked equally low by anglers. Canadian authorities have been unable to differentiate two species within their waters. This may indicate that only one of the two are found there. Research seems to favor the premise that the white hake is that species which is found within Canadian boundaries.

Atlantic Cod
Gadus morhua

Local Names:

- Rock Cod
- Codfish
- Morue Commune
- Cabillaud

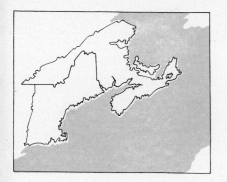

Distinguishing Characteristics:

- Has three, soft, rayed dorsals and two soft, rayed analfins
- Has no spines in any of its fins
- Heavy bodied, especially beneath the first dorsal
- A large head, being about one-fourth of the fish's total length
- Chin barbel
- Body is sprinkled with dark spots

Average Size:

- 1-3 feet (0.30-0.91 m.)
- 5-20 pounds (2-9 kg.)

Habits:

- May be found at any depth, but prefers to remain on or near the bottom
- Is sometimes taken from the surf along our beaches, especially in the fall of the year
- Usually found over rocky or gravelly bottoms
- Feeds on herring and other fishes, but the main source of food is mollusks such as clams, mussels, and welks; these are generally taken whole

The Atlantic cod has been such an important part of the New England commercial fishery that a carving of a very large cod still hangs on display in

101

the Massachusetts State House. As soon as the first white settlers became established in the New World, they began the long development of this vast fishery. At that time, cod were generally butterfly dressed — salted and hung on large racks to dry in the sun. In fact, cod preserved in this manner is still available from most specialty food markets. Most of the fish marketed this way comes from Scotland and Scandinavia.

Probably all the seafaring nations of the North Atlantic have at one time relied heavily on the prolific cod as an important source of food. Several methods are employed in harvesting this fish. The most common method, used by local small-boat fishermen, is the drag net. The net is taken to the ocean floor by heavy chains attached to its bottom leading edge. It is held open horizontally by a pair of "doors," which plane outward at each front corner. The net is held open vertically by round plastic or metal buoys set at regular intervals along the top leading edge. When the rig reaches the bottom, it is dragged over an area where fish are suspected to be gathered. Fish are moved from the bottom as the net reaches them and as they are overtaken, they move toward the much smaller "bag" at the rear end of the net.

Another cod fishing method is the long line, This consists of a series of baited hooks secured to a long, heavy line, which is anchored at each end and marked by surface buoys. The line may be set for any length of time, usually one to three days. At the end of the desired period, the line is hauled aboard and the fish removed from the hooks.

A third method for taking large numbers of fish is the mid-water trawl. This net is similar to the drag, but it rides higher in the water and can therefore be used in areas where a rocky or uneven ground would ruin the bottom drag.

With the increasing popularity of sport fishing from "party" or head boats, the cod has gained prominence as a game fish. A very large percentage of the annual party-boat catch is cod. This has been increasingly true in recent years, as the haddock stocks have been severely depleted by over harvesting.

Atlantic cod are most often taken on whole or cut fish bait or heavy metal jigs, which are bounced close to the bottom. Fish from fifteen to thirty pounds are not uncommon on any party-boat trip. Boats returning from a day of ground fishing will often carry five hundred to six hundred pounds of fish in their holds. Cod are considered very good table fish; as evidence, the vast commercial fishery for this species. Their flesh is, however, not as firm as that of the haddock and in warm months is often infested with small, red worms.

Anglers working the surf for striped bass or bluefish will take an occasional cod, especially in the autumn when these fish are often in shallow water.

Atlantic Tomcod

Microgadus tomcod

Local Names:

- Frost Fish
- Pelite Morue
- Loche

Distinguishing Characteristics:

- The ventral fins are much longer than those of the cod and taper to a very definite filament, suggesting a feeler rather than the usual fin shape
- The caudal fin is decidedly rounded, whereas the cod's is square or slightly concave
- The head and eye are smaller than those of the cod
- The margin of the first anal fin is rounded

Average Size:

- 9-15 inches (23-38 cm.)
- ½-1¼ pounds (0.22-0.67 kg.)

Habits:

- Limited to inshore waters; rarely encountered more than a mile from shore
- Found in estuaries and shallow mud-bottom bays and harbors
- Often taken from brackish water and in streams in winter months
- Leave the estuaries in the spring for somewhat cooler water slightly offshore, to return again in the fall
- Feed primarily on shrimp, worms, squid, and smaller fishes such as mummichogs, launce, silversides, and smelt

Commercially unimportant because of their relative scarcity compared with the larger Atlantic cod, very few of these small fish find their way to market. They are, however, very good eating. Tomcod provide some degree of sport to the inshore fisherman. However, they are not usually sought but are occasionally taken by anglers fishing for mackerel, pollock, or striped bass. However, tomcod do contribute to a rather large market as bait. Used primarily by ice fishermen seeking trout, salmon, and pickerel, tomcod (small specimens averaging 3 to 5 inches in length) are favored because they are extremely hardy and withstand a great deal of neglect and wide temperature fluctuations.

Burbot

Lota lota

Local Names:

- Ling
- Eelpout
- Cusk
- Freshwater Cod
- Lotte

Distinguishing Characteristics:

- Single chin barbel on lower jaw
- Elongated rather eel-like body

- Very long soft rayed second dorsal preceded by short soft rayed first dorsal
- Small rounded caudal fin
- Large head and mouth
- Ventral fins terminate in short thread-like projections

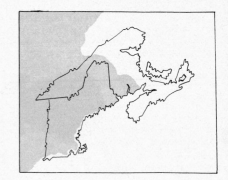

Average Size:

- 12-20 inches (31-51 cm.)
- 1-5 pounds (0.45-2 kg.)

Habits:

- Occurs in large, deep, cold lakes, preferring habitat indentical to that of the lake trout
- Spawning occurs in mid-winter under the ice
- The burbot is generally a bottom feeder (especially in the warm summer months. However, when the water is cool, it roams widely throughout the lakes.

This fish is not given much attention by either sport or commercial fishermen. In fact, since it consumes large quantities of smaller fishes (game fishes included), it is usually considered a nuisance. The burbot is most often taken by anglers ice-fishing for other species.

The quality of the burbot as a food fish seems never to have been agreed upon. However, it is nowhere highly regarded as table fare.

Anyone wishing to catch one of these predators would be advised to consider the fish's habits as similar to those of the eel; and to fish for it close to the bottom of our deeper lakes.

Haddock
Melanogrammus aeglefinus

Distinguishing Characteristics:

- Very similar to cod in fin arrangement and general body shape
- Unlike the cod, in which the reverse is true, the haddock has a black or dark lateral line on a light ground
- The first dorsal is much higher than the second two and tapers to a sharp point

110

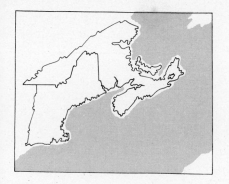

- A dark patch, known as the "devil's mark," is positioned just above the pectorals
- Caudal fin is more deeply concave than in the cod
- Chin barbel is quite short

Average Size:

- 14-24 inches (36-61 cm.)
- 3-6 pounds (1-3 kg.)

Habits:

- Generally found in deeper water than cod, the haddock is almost never taken in shallow water near shore
- Can tolerate a smaller temperature range than the cod
- Remains close to bottom at all times and very seldom will they pursue prey into shallower water, as is the case with the cod
- Haddock prefer smooth, hard bottoms among rocky areas

For so many years the haddock has been considered "the" food fish on the Eastern seaboard that recent declines in their stocks have radically altered the world's fish market. The newly enacted 200-mile United States fishing limit resulted largely from the heavy tolls of haddock taken by foreign vessels. This was at one time an extremely numerous species, comprising a very large percentage of the annual commercial and sport-fishing catch. Party-boat catches would often have more haddock than cod. Presently, however, it is an

111

unusual day when any haddock are taken at all. These alarming facts are ample evidence that the once-common belief that the sea would provide endless fish stocks for man's indiscriminate use is simply not true. It will be many years hence before the haddock will return to any semblance of its original numbers.

Haddock are taken commercially by the same methods used for taking cod. Anglers will find them taking worms, cut fish, clams, and many other baits worked along the bottom. Like the cod, the haddock is not very game on the line. But it will give a fairly strong fight on medium spinning or casting tackle as it pulls toward the bottom. The prime attraction of this fish is its excellent table qualities. Fish and chips, finnan haddie, fish chowder, and many processed forms of haddock are available, and they are all delicious when properly prepared using fresh fish. The meat is white, firm, and very flaky. It is little wonder that this species has been so heavily harvested.

All the ground fish, and their population variations, are responsible for the economic success or failure of the Atlantic coast fishing fleet. It is hoped that regulation and improvement of management techniques will save the haddock from eventual extinction.

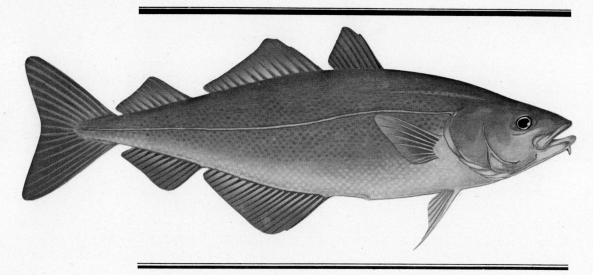

American Pollock

Pollachius virens

Local Names:

- Boston Bluefish
- Merlan Noire
- Colin

Distinguishing Characteristics:

- The body tends to be deeper overall than that of the cod or haddock
- Lower jaw protrudes beyond the upper

- Ventral fins are smaller than in the cod or haddock
- The chin barbel is very small
- Caudal fin is deeply concave, almost forked
- Light lateral line on darker ground
- The back is an attractive olive green, varying very little among individuals

Average Size:

- 14-30 inches (36-76 cm.)
- 1½-10 pounds (0.67-4 kg.)

Habits:

- Will follow available food to any depth from a deep bottom on the one hand to shallow bays, harbors, and estuaries
- Often found schooling with mackerel
- Feeds primarily on small schooling fishes, but also favors shrimp and squid when available
- Young pollock are usually found in harbors, estuaries, and browsing in the weed beds of the intertidal zone

Pollock are so plentiful and so voracious that anyone who has fished along any of our coasts has probably encountered large numbers of these attractive fish. Pollock are almost always taken by anglers working to hook mackerel, striped bass, bluefish, or any of the ground fish. They are usually met in large schools, which are rather loosely formed when close to shore. These are strong fighting fish and will make a good accounting of themselves when taken on light or even ultralight tackle.

When in shoal water or rivers and bays, pollock are frequently seen charging schools of sand launce. When so engaged, these active fish will often jump clear of the water or splash violently with their tails, leaving hundreds of telltale "boils" on the surface. Casting a medium-sized streamer fly of any description into a feeding school will produce immediate action. Pollock will often chase a fly or lure for a sizeable distance before actually being hooked. Their behavior in shallow water superficially resembles that of our freshwater trouts. A few hours of casting flies over pollock is an excellent way for the trout fisher to hone his skills of accurate casting and striking.

Any number of other baits or lures will take these fish. Small spinners, jigs, light swimming plugs, and surface lures will all produce action. And the bait fisherman will find pollock quite willing to devour sea worms, clams, cut fish, or small live bait.

The flesh of the pollock is not nearly as white or as firm as that of the haddock or cod. Many fishermen either release them or simply do not eat them because of this. However, many people do find them quite appetizing, especially in chowder. With haddock in short supply, more and more pollock are finding their way to market as fresh or frozen substitutes.

Flatfishes

Local Names:

- Blackback
- Lemon Sole

Winter Flounder

Pseudopleuronectes americanus

- Mud Dab
- Black Flounder
- Carulet

Distinguishing Characteristics:

- Eyes on right side
- Small mouth
- Lateral line is nearly straight

Average Size:

- 12-18 inches (31-46 cm.)
- 1-5 pounds (0.45-2 kg.)

Habits:

- Frequent waters from the intertidal zone to as deep as forty to fifty fathoms
- Often found in estuaries and river mouths, occasionally entering the lower reaches of fresh water
- Does not appear to migrate at all
- Fish found close to shore are usually on sand or muddy sand, while in deeper water they are found on hard bottoms
- Feed by darting out from hiding (usually buried in sand or mud) to intercept fish or shrimp

117

- Concentrations of these fish move into and away from certain areas to remain within a comfortable temperature range

It goes without saying that the flounders are all bottom fishes, but the winter flounder seems more closely attached to the ground than some other members of its tribe. This fish usually lies almost completely buried in mud, sand, or gravel, with nothing but its eyes exposed. Flounders are some of our most stationary fishes, moving about very little except when feeding. Their extremely well camouflaged bodies become almost indistinguishable from the ground as they lie in wait for unsuspecting prey. Winter flounder feed primarily on shrimp, squid, and small fishes.

Of prime importance as commercial fishes, the flounders also make fine game fishes. Their flattened bodies serve very well as planing surfaces as they struggle to regain the bottom.

Flounders will take a wide assortment of baits, but they show a marked preference for sea worms (mud worms). They have, however, been known to strike artificial lures fished near the bottom. They have even been taken (on rare occasion) by fly fishermen working tidal water for other species. The flesh of these bottom fish is white, firm, and very "sweet" tasting. There are many ways to serve flounder (usually referred to as sole.) The fine flavor of these usually small species is their prime attraction for fishermen. However, a peaceful day in a boat on calm inshore waters is a most enjoyable way in which to spend one's time.

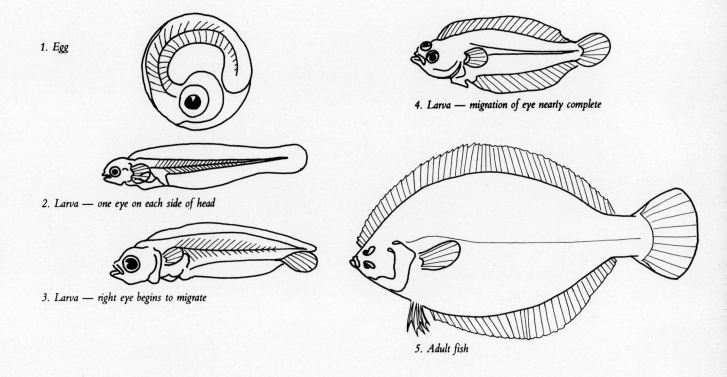

1. *Egg*

2. *Larva — one eye on each side of head*

3. *Larva — right eye begins to migrate*

4. *Larva — migration of eye nearly complete*

5. *Adult fish*

Physical Development of Winter
Flounder, *Pseudopleuronectes americanus*

119

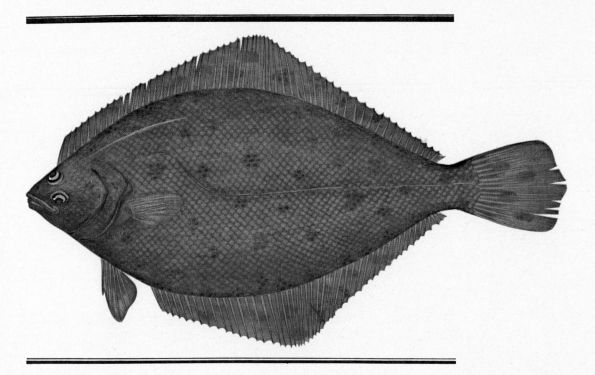

Local Names:

- Flounder
- Fluke
- Plaicefish
- Doormat Fluke

Summer Flounder

Paralichthys dentatus

Distinguishing Characteristics:

- Eyes on left side of head
- Large head and mouth
- The body is narrower than that of the winter flounder

Average Size:

- 17-26 inches (43-66 cm.)
- 2-8 pounds (0.91-4 kg.)

Habits:

- A more southerly fish than the winter flounder
- More active in its pursuit of prey than the winter flounder, frequently chasing schools of small fish to the surface
- When in shoal water, summer flounder are usually found on sandy or mud bottoms

Important information about the summer flounder is nearly identical to that for the winter flounder with only slight variations. These differences occur primarily in the ranges of the two fishes. The summer flounder (or fluke) is generally a fish of more southerly waters. The tip of Cape Cod at Provincetown is usually the northernmost area from which these fish are taken. They are, however, quite common along the coasts of Rhode Island, Connecticut, and New York, where they are highly regarded as both commercial and game fish.

121

Local Names:

- Halibut

Distinguishing Characteristics:

- Large size
- A relatively narrow body with a large head and mouth

Atlantic Halibut

Hippoglossus hippoglossus

- Caudal fin is markedly concave
- Eyes on right side of head

Average Size:

- 4-6 feet (1-2 m.)
- 50-200 pounds (23-91 kg.)

Habits:

- Usually found on grounds of sand or other hard material
- A very strong and active ground fish
- Smaller fish are found in shallower water and larger in deeper water

The halibut is not, strictly speaking, a game fish. Its major importance is as a commercial species. However, these often very large and always very strong ground fish are occasionally taken by anglers in search of other bottom-dwelling fishes, especially cod or haddock. They are usually in reach of coastal sport fishermen in the spring or early summer, when they return to somewhat shallower water during the warmer months of the year. Halibut are present along our coasts throughout the summer, but they are rather slow to take a hook. They are taken primarily in April and May, because dogfish have not moved inshore at that time and do not compete for the fisherman's bait.

The halibut is prized as a commercial species, its flesh being very firm and mild in flavor. These great fish are usually cut into "steaks" about one-inch thick and marketed fresh or frozen.

Anadromous - Catadromous

Atlantic Sturgeon
Acipenser sturio

Local Names:

- Sea Sturgeon
- American Sturgeon

Distinguishing Characteristics:

- A long, shovel-like snout with four longish barbels ahead of the mouth

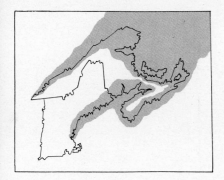

- Small, inferior mouth used for sucking food from bottom
- Three rows of hard, bony plates — one dorsal, one ventral, and one lateral

Average Size:

- 6-10 feet (2-3.05 m.)
- 60-250 pounds (27-113 kg.)

Habits:

- Anadromous, entering fresh water in late spring to spawn
- A bottom feeder, grubbing in mud and sand for worms, mollusks, occasionally taking small fishes, especially sand launce
- These great fish are occasionally seen making high leaps from the water

Being an anadromous fish (living most of its life at sea and returning to its native streams to spawn), the sturgeon has suffered greatly from the damming and pollution of our major rivers. The sturgeon is included here because of the great numbers of them that were encountered up to about 25 years ago. Today, fishermen sight an occasional large fish jumping clear of the water. These sightings usually occur in the estuaries of rivers where anglers congregate to fish for striped bass.

The history of the decline of this valuable fish is a carbon copy of the decline of the Atlantic salmon, the shad, and the alewife. The only slight difference is that no effort is being made to restore the stocks of sturgeon. We can only hope that when our rivers do see major improvements, these fish will return to their spawning beds and naturally recoup their losses.

A major factor in the neglect of the sturgeon is its low standing on the average fisherman's list of most-sought fishes. But a fish of this size would certainly be a challenge on medium or light tackle. In years past, during times when sturgeon were quite plentiful, they were sought primarily by commercial fishermen for their roe (caviar), oil, and flesh. Restoration of the Atlantic sturgeon to our waters could provide a resurgence in a market that has been allowed to lie fallow for too many years.

Lake Sturgeon
Acipenser fulvescens

Local Names:

- Rock Sturgeon
- Sturgeon
- Red Sturgeon
- Smoothback
- Esturgeon de Lac

Distinguishing Characteristics:

- Very similar to the Atlantic sturgeon, but skin is smoother with fewer bony protuberances

129

- Skin becomes increasingly smooth with age, so that adult fish show only remnants of the bony plates

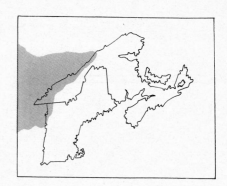

Average Size:

- 3-5 feet (0.91-2 m.)
- 10-80 pounds (5-36 kg.)

Habits:

- Occurs in large, deep lakes and rivers
- Ascends rivers and streams (where available) to spawn. Will spawn on gravel or sand in shallow, wave-washed waters where rivers are not available

The lake sturgeon has had a very interesting and varied history in its relation to man (one of its very few predators.) During the early 1800s, the lake sturgeon was considered a nuisance and trash fish. During this period, it was used as food for pigs and dogs. It was dried and used as fuel for steam ships, or simply killed and thrown overboard, or dried and burned. Several Indian tribes were at that time well aware of the fine flavor of this great fish. They were very happy to have the white man regard the lake sturgeon as worthless. But by mid-century the white man realized the lake sturgeon for what it was, a fine food fish with many valuable assets, including its roe as caviar, its swim bladder, which yielded gelatin isinglass (used to clarify wine and beer), and its

130

skin, which was occasionally tanned. Since then the commercial value of the lake sturgeon has continued to rise by leaps and bounds.

Those who can afford it are very glad to pay the premium price for smoked sturgeon or caviar. Unfortunately, the high price reflects a distinct shortage of the commodity. When fishermen first realized the value of this species, over a century ago, the boom was on and vast numbers of this slow-growing fish were harvested. The lake sturgeon has never been able to recover from that onslaught, combined with pollution and destruction of its spawning beds. Perhaps the efforts to clean up our once-pure North American environment will give this fine fish a fighting chance to make a comeback.

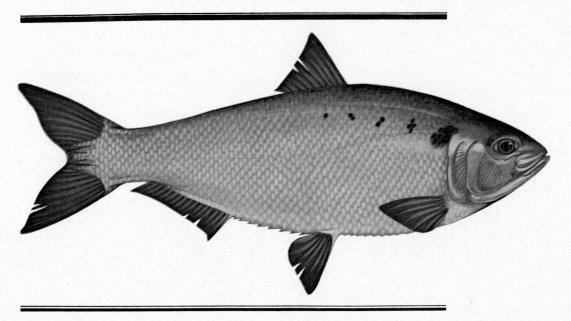

American Shad

Alosa sapidissima

Local Names:

- Shad
- White Shad
- Jack
- Atlantic Shad

132

Alewife
Alosa pseudoharengus

Local Names:

- Gaspereau
- Sawbelly
- Shad
- Pogy

Distinguishing Characteristics:

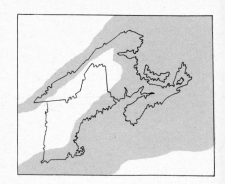

- Very similar to *A. sapidissima,* but generally runs smaller and is less robust
- Body is strongly compressed laterally
- Anal fin is shorter than in the shad, having 16 to 20 rays, compared to the former's 30 to 32

Average Size:

- 6-10 inches (15-25 cm.)
- ½-1 pound (0.22-0.45 kg.)

Habits:

- Most common in salt water, ascending streams and rivers to spawn
- Occurs naturally as a landlocked species in many areas and has been introduced as a potential forage fish in some watersheds
- A schooling fish that often travels in very large numbers

The alewife is not generally considered a game fish and is included here only because it is a well-known species, is often used for bait, and is easily confused with the shad.

For many years, live alewives have been the favorite bait of anglers in search of bluefish. In fact, the occurrence of bluefish in Gulf of Maine waters seems closely tied to the availability of large numbers of this forage fish. As bait, they are usually fished live, hooked through the back and allowed to drift on the running tide.

Alewives have some minor commercial value but are usually processed into fish meal. The flesh is sweet tasting, but quite bony.

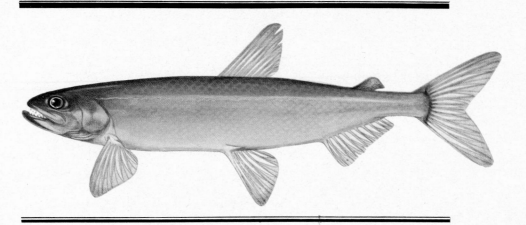

Rainbow Smelt
Osmerus mordax

Local Names:

- American Smelt
- Smelt
- Leefish
- Frostfish
- Icefish
- Freshwater Smelt
- Eperlan Arc-en-Ciel

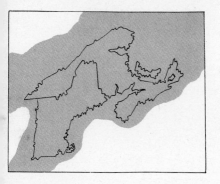

Distinguishing Characteristics:

- Elongated, slender body
- Deeply forked caudal fin
- Large mouth with upper jawbone (maxillary) extending beyond the rear margin of the eye
- The small average size of this fish serves as a generally reliable field identification

Average Size:

- 4-8 inches (10-20 cm.)
- 5-10 ounces (118-236 mlg.)

Habits:

- A schooling fish providing a staple in the diet of larger fresh- and salt water game fishes
- Occurs in fresh, salt, and brackish waters throughout its range
- In salt and brackish water, it is usually found near the surface in relatively shallow water; in fresh water it will generally be found at depths favored by our cold-water species, although populations are established in many warm, shallow-water habitats
- Schools tend to wander throughout the year from warm to cool water temperatures

139

- Spawning takes place in early spring, when large numbers of these usually small fish swarm up nearly any available source of running water

Rainbow smelt or just plain smelt (in most of their range) are important as forage for larger fish, as a prime bait fish, and as a delicacy on the table. Because of its wide and varied uses, the smelt is one of our most important (though often overlooked) fishes. The most common method used for taking these fine fish is to dip them from their spawning streams with a long-handled fine-mesh net. Smelt spawn at night (usually around midnight or later), and smelting parties are a favorite occupation of winter-weary sportsmen in our ranges. During these outings, a good deal of alcohol is generally consumed (allegedly for the purpose of warming the body on a chilly spring evening). On a good night of smelting, the fisherman will be rewarded with several quarts of smelts, good companionship, and (often) little memory of the whole experience.

Ice fishing in brackish water is another favorite method for taking smelts. Under adverse conditions, this can be a risky business as tide changes have been known to move ice fishermen, fishing gear, and ice shanties a considerable distance. But, whether the season is winter or spring, smelt fishermen are often fanatic in their devotion to this delicious little fish.

Smelt are easy to prepare for cooking — remove the head and entrails, dipping the whole fish in egg batter and cracker crumbs or corn meal, then quickly frying in deep fat or a greased skillet results in a delightful meal in which the smaller fish are consumed whole.

American Eel

Anguilla rostrata

Local Names:

- Atlantic Eel
- Eel
- Common Eel
- Silver Eel
- Freshwater Eel
- Easgann
- Anquille d' Amerique

141

Distinguishing Characteristics:

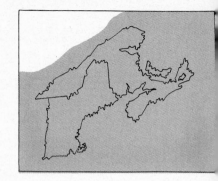

- The American eel can be mistaken for no other fish common to our range
- The long, snake-like body with one long fin running along the rear two-thirds of the body are enough to set the American eel apart from other fishes

Average Size:

- 18-36 inches (46-91 cm.)
- 1-5 pounds (0.45-2 kg.)

Habits:

- The eel is catadromous, meaning that it lives primarily in fresh water and returns to salt water to spawn
- All eels are born in the Sargasso Sea, an area of the Atlantic Ocean off Bermuda that supports a dense growth of seaweed (*sargassum*)
- Young eels enter fresh water and move upstream in the spring
- Males usually remain in brackish or salt water, while females continue upstream
- Females may remain in fresh water for many years before returning to the sea to spawn
- Eels inhabit all types of water within their range, from clear, cold lakes to nearly stagnant, warm, shallow pools

142

- Found in fast or slow water
- Can survive for short periods away from water and will sometimes hunt for food on damp or wet areas near its home

The eel is such an interesting fish that many scientific works have been devoted to its habits and life history. As a game fish, its reputation is by no means the best.

Eels have for many centuries been captured for food. The European markets buy and sell many tons of these fish each year. Because they are best when eaten fresh, eels are often found alive in the marketplace. This is less true in North America, where our taste for refined foods has taken us far away from the old-fashioned fishmonger's cries. Nevertheless, this fish still finds its way in large numbers to U.S. and Canadian markets. It is most often sold after it has been smoked or pickled.

An angler wishing to catch his own eel dinner will have little trouble doing so. Any bait will do, since the eel is a well-known scavenger. Because of their availability and ease of capture, earthworms are most often used as bait for eels. The eel is a nocturnal creature, and the angler's success will be greatly increased if he keeps this in mind. However, good catches of eels are often made during the day, since they are voracious feeders and seem always to be hungry. Any serviceable fishing rod is adequate; in fact, many fishermen prefer to use handlines. A sinker is necessary, since this fish is a bottom feeder. The hook may be large or small, but the bait is more likely to be taken if it tends towards the larger sizes.

Eels are surprisingly strong and will make a good accounting of themselves, especially on light tackle. There always seems to be large numbers of this fish wherever it is found, so the angler can fish unrestricted until he has had his fill.

Along our coasts where striped bass are the favorite game fish, live eels are often the best bait for *M. saxatilis.* When used as bait, eels from 6 to 12 inches (15.24-30.48 cm.) in length are carefully hooked through the back and allowed to drift on the running tide. Each season many of the largest striped bass are taken in this manner.

Fresh Water

Salmonoids, Salmons, and Trouts

Atlantic Salmon
Salmo salar

Local Names:

- Salmon
- Saumon Atlantique

146

Distinguishing Characteristics:

- Long, slender body and small, pointed head
- Dark x-shaped or irregular black spots sprinkled on back above the lateral line
- Small mouth with short upper jaw

Average Size:

- 18-30 inches (46-76 cm.)
- 5-15 pounds (2-7 kg.)

Habits:

- Anadromous, living and feeding primarily at sea, returning to the freshwater streams of its birth to spawn
- Roams widely while at sea, generally close to shore; found to congregate in the area of the Davis Strait off Greenland, where heavy commercial fishing has drastically reduced its world population
- While in fresh water, these fish are usually found holding at the heads or tails of deeper pools in fast-moving rivers
- Great controversy has surrounded the question of the salmon's feeding habits while in fresh water. Stomachs of salmon taken in fresh water have always been found to be empty, but salmon are often seen in pursuit of bait fish

• While at sea, salmon feed mainly on shrimp or prawn, small fishes (such as alewives or silversides), and squid when available

Within our range, the Atlantic salmon is rightfully known as the "king of game fish." For the fly-fishing enthusiast, the Atlantic salmon has traditionally been, and will probably continue to be, "the" fish.

In North America, sport fishing for salmon is restricted by law to the use of fly fishing equipment with only a few exceptions. A great mystique has grown around this fish and the fabled waters from which it is still taken. A great sum of money is spent each year by fishermen in search of this fish. Most of that money is spent in the localities where salmon can still be found. This influx of money is a great boon to the communities where anglers gather. For this reason, government officials, both on the national and local level, are becoming increasingly aware of the salmon's economic value as a sport rather than a commercial resource. It has been estimated that visiting sportsmen pay as much as $100.00 per pound for each Atlantic salmon they take. When compared with the $4.00 to $5.00 per pound that salmon brings on the commercial market, it is easy to see that a strictly protected sport fishery for this once-abundant fish is much more profitable than an open commercial fishery.

During the century just past, salmon were so common that, in one tributary of the Kennebec River in Maine, they were speared during their spawning run and used as fertilizer for the nearby corn and bean fields. There were, in fact, laws prohibiting owners of logging camps and other labor-intensive businesses from serving salmon more than three times per week. There are today, to be sure, many ardent salmon fishers who would pay enormous sums of money merely to cast a fly over a salmon, let alone to be served salmon even once a week.

The decline of the Atlantic salmon, the American shad, the sturgeon, and many other anadromous fishes is only one example of man's unhappy history as a despoiler of his own planet. These great fish are victims of our thoughtless rush into the industrial/technological age in which we live. Surrounded now by the seemingly boundless fruits of our industrial/technological labors, we have gained enough leisure time to reflect on what we have achieved. There are many who, in retrospect, would have gladly sacrificed at least one technological milestone for a mere chance to take a fresh-run Atlantic salmon from a clear, free-flowing stream.

Fortunately, the stocks of salmon have not been so depleted as to be hopeless. In fact, all the governments within our range have taken admirable steps toward restoring the salmon to a semblance of its original numbers. Great rivers, which once supported vast numbers of salmon, such as the Connecticut, the Merrimack, and the Penobscot, are now being given the attention required by such a massive project as this. The Penobscot in Maine is perhaps the most exciting as a suggestion that under even less than optimum conditions the Atlantic salmon will oblige in doing its share in the job of restoration. In this, and many smaller rivers, hatchery-reared salmon are proving that the creation of passageways over dams and pollution abatement will pay high dividends on a continuing basis. Perhaps the future of this wonderful fish will be much brighter than its recent past.

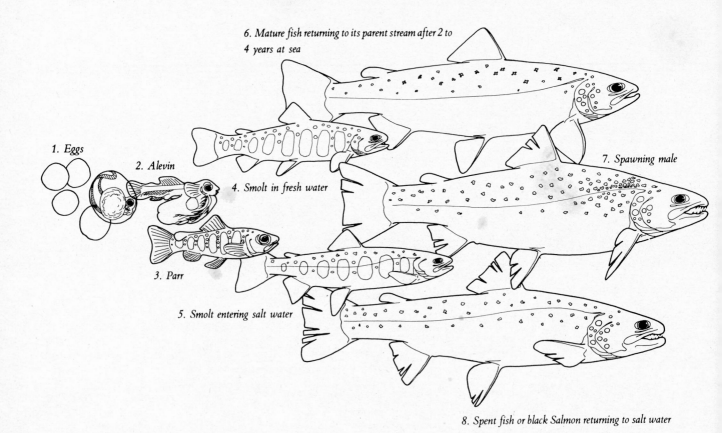

6. *Mature fish returning to its parent stream after 2 to 4 years at sea*

1. *Eggs*

2. *Alevin*

4. *Smolt in fresh water*

3. *Parr*

5. *Smolt entering salt water*

7. *Spawning male*

8. *Spent fish or black Salmon returning to salt water*

Life Cycle of the Atlantic Salmon,
Salmo salar
150

Landlocked Salmon

Salmo salar (sebago)

Local Names:

- Sebago Salmon
- Ouananiche

Distinguishing Characteristics:

- Anatomically identical to the sea-run Atlantic salmon
- Since landlocked Atlantic salmon run smaller than sea-run fish, they usually have a shallow fork in the median of the caudal fin

Average Size:

- 12-24 inches (30-61 cm.)
- 1-5 pounds (0.45-2 kg.)

Habits:

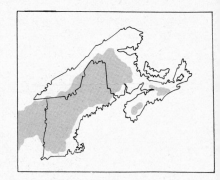

- Usually found in deep, cold lakes, where certain depths remain within the 50 to 55 degree F (10 to 12 degree C.) range throughout the warmer months
- In the spring of the year when lakes are homogenized or turning over, salmon come to the surface to feed on smelt and other forage fishes
- Found in tributaries and thoroughfares of larger lakes, especially in the spring and fall
- Some large freshwater rivers maintain good stocks of salmon throughout the season. In such waters, fish are found at the head and tail of deeper pools and shallow, whitewater sections

It has been shown recently that there is no structural difference between sea-run and landlocked specimens of this fish. But, because our region (especially Maine) is the world center of the landlocked salmon's population, it is here given special attention, enough to merit separating it from the sea-run fish for the purpose of study.

As the sea-run fish is truly "the" game fish, especially for fly-fishermen, so the landlocked salmon may well be the king of the waters away from the

152

salt. Every spring as the ice goes off our deep, cold lakes, anglers are found trolling streamer flies (originated in Maine for the purpose of taking salmon and brook trout) or live smelts in hopes of catching salmon as they cruise near the surface feeding on smelts and other forage fish. This is normally the prime time for salmon fishing. Fly patterns such as the Grey Ghost, Green Ghost, Supervisor, and many others, tied on tandem or long-shank single hooks, are responsible for the majority of salmon taken early in the season. As the water warms, these fish seek out the 50- to 55-degree temperature range most favorable to their lifestyle. To find this specific temperature range, salmon must continue to drop to greater depths — often to 50 or 70 feet (14.63 to 22.86 m.) Here they can be taken by using a wire or lead-core line, which greatly reduces the fish's ability to give its usually spectacular show of acrobatics. One alternative to leaded or wire lines is the increasingly popular "down-rigger" system. With this deep-trolling rig, a light trolling or spinning line is clipped onto a quick-release mechanism attached to a heavy weight. The weight, which is often torpedo shaped, is secured to the boat by a line connected to a large reel-type device. This rig, because of its weight, follows nearly directly under the boat when fished at trolling speed. When a fish takes the lure or bait, the fishing line is instantly released from the weight and the angler is then free to play the fish on a light line.

Landlocked salmon have deep pink or orange flesh of excellent flavor. They may be baked, broiled, smoked, or poached, all of which will provide a fine meal for the fortunate fisherman and his family.

Coho Salmon
Oncorhynchus kisutch

Local Names:

- Coho
- Salmon
- Silver Salmon

Distinguishing Characteristics:

- Generally a deeper bodied fish than the Atlantic salmon, although young specimens closely resemble *Salmo salar*

154

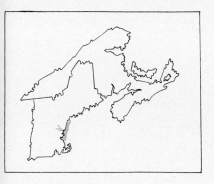

- Head and mouth are larger than in Atlantic salmon (except in young fish)
- The most reliable differentiating field mark between the Coho and the Atlantic is the number of rays in the anal fin. The coho has thirteen or more of these rays, while Atlantic salmon have eleven or less, as do the sea-run brook trout or sea-run brown trout

Average Size:

- 20-30 inches (51-76 cm.)
- 5-12 pounds (2-5 kg.)

Habits:

- Identical to those of the Atlantic salmon, except that cohos die after spawning, while Atlantic salmon may spawn as many as three or four times

The coho salmon is a native of the coasts of the northern Pacific Ocean. In recent years its range has been extended through some very successful plantings (notably in the Great Lakes region). It occurs within our range only as a locally abundant species. The center of its population is in the waters in and around Great Bay and the Piscataqua River in New Hampshire. Experimental stocking began in the Exeter and Lamprey Rivers, which flow into Great Bay, in 1969. The returns have been consistent and fairly heavy since that time. It is not known how many fish are actually surviving as

155

offspring from hatchery-reared parents, but a small fishery has developed for this fish in that locality.

The coho salmon may well provide sportsmen (and eventually commercial fishermen) with a viable alternative to Atlantic salmon in waters where the latter may not succeed. However, there is strong opposition among many devoted Atlantic salmon anglers to the introduction of this exotic fish.

The coho salmon is, however, a fine food and game fish, growing to an average of ten to twelve pounds (4.54-5.45 kg.) in three years. If the Great Lakes restoration (based on coho and chinook salmon) is an indication of the potential of these great fishes, then we are likely to see many more experimental stockings of coho salmon in the near future.

Brown Trout

Salmo trutta

Local Names:

- Brownie
- German Brown

Distinguishing Characteristics:

- Large size, often with a long, rather large head
- Red spots haloed by white along flanks

157

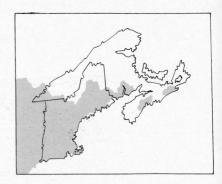

- Distinctly rounded fins, especially the paired fins and the tail

Average Size:

- 10-18 inches (25-46 cm.)
- 1-8 pounds (0.45-4 kg.)

Habits:

- Large, deep rivers
- Small, well-oxygenated streams (spawning)
- Large lakes and ponds
- Where possible the brown trout will run to the sea

It is now well known that the brown trout was not originally found anywhere in North America. During the 1880s this trout was introduced into some ponds in eastern Maine. Its debut was regarded by many sportsmen as an intrusion on the easy brook trout fishing that they were enjoying at that time. In the Northeast, where good populations of native brook trout still remain, this sentiment persists even today. But in waters where brook trout habitat has been severely altered, the brown trout provides food and sport that might otherwise not be available at all. It is true that, pound for pound, the brown trout is much more difficult to catch than either the brook trout or the rainbow trout. Because of what seems to be a superior intelligence, this fish

158

often survives longer than the other trouts and therefore provides a stock of much larger fish.

The problem faced by the fisherman is how to capture these wise old browns. At certain times of the year, large aquatic insects, such as stone flies and the larger mayflies, can be found hatching in clear-running streams. In the predominantly freestone streams of New England and eastern Canada, these hatches offer the dry-fly fisherman his best chances to take large brown trout. Generally, however, a good-sized streamer or wet fly fished along the bottom of deep pools and glides will provide more consistant sport. Since the brown trout is much more active at night, it is often recommended that the angler be on his favorite stream after dark. Each season many five-pound and larger browns are taken by fishermen drifting night crawlers through deep river pools. It is advisable to know a stream very well before attempting to wade at night. A sunny riffle seen in the morning can become a dangerous piece of whitewater by night.

Probably the easiest way to catch brown trout is to troll streamer flies, spinning lures, or live bait after ice-out in the spring. Like all fish living in deep, cold lakes, brown trout will be on or near the surface at the time when these waters are turning over. Some of the largest browns may be taken in this way.

Brown Trout (sea-run)

Salmo trutta

Local Names:

- Sea Trout
- Salter

Distinguishing Characteristics:

- Proportionately smaller head than average freshwater specimens
- Caudal fin is more squared than in landlocked fish

160

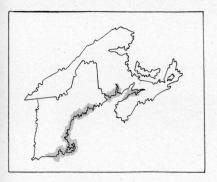

- Silvery coloration resembling that of salmons
- May be distinguished from salmon by the presence of red spots on flanks. Usually retains red margin on adipose fin

Average Size:

- 14-18 inches (36-46 cm.)
- 2-6 pounds (0.91-3 kg.)

Habits:

- Enters salt water wherever available
- Some populations may contain sea-run as well as non sea-run fish
- Never encountered far from shore; usually restricted to estuaries and nearby areas of the open ocean
- Congregate in pools at the head of tide, where they begin the fall spawning migration
- Feed on small marine crustaceans and mollusks as well as bait fish such as sand launce, silversides, and mummichogs

Wherever they are found, sea-run trout provide an almost exotic bonus to the regular fare of salt- or freshwater fishing. They are trout and maintain all the fine fighting and eating qualities of their freshwater lives, but they gain weight and stamina in the marine environment. Since the diet of sea-run trout is composed primarily of fish, they are somewhat less selective than the same species found in freshwater. But, what they loose in finesse during their saltwater migrations, they more than regain in strength and beauty. Sea-run brown trout become more salmon-like in their appearance than our other sea-trout. Their flanks turn a bright silver, and their dark spots become smaller. The tell-tale red spots remain and serve as a reliable identification mark. The rapid growth rate encouraged by heavy feeding while at sea produces a fish with a more pointed, smaller head than is usual in freshwater specimens.

Few populations of sea-trout are harvested to anywhere near their full potential. In the case of the sea-run brown trout, spawning runs begin in mid-to-late fall and continue until mid-winter. This creates a sometimes chilling situation for the angler. But, with some warm clothing, a calm day, and a knowledge of the fish and its habitat, the hardy angler can often find himself in a fishing paradise.

A typical sea-trout fishing scenario would have a lone fisherman wading a tide marsh, surrounded by the dull browns and greens of the grasses, with a backdrop of brilliant fall foliage and a hazy blue sky. For companions, migrating Canada geese, black ducks, buffleheads, and goldeneyes would complete the picture. The simple streamer flies tied to the end of a light- to medium-leader tippet would attract strong decisive strikes from active fish in the two- to six-pound class. Holding with these chunky browns would be the occasional sea-run brook trout, which only adds to the excitement.

There are many streams of varying size draining directly into the sea all along the New England and Canadian Atlantic coast. Many of these waters support large, healthy populations of sea-trout, which are generally ignored by all but dyed-in-the-wool fishermen.

Rainbow Trout

Salmo gairdneri

Distinguishing Characteristics:

- Small black spots covering sides and upper body
- Head is usually shorter and more blunt than in either the brown or the brook trout
- A pronounced pink stripe usually runs the length of the body
- The body is deeper from the dorsal fin to the belly than the other trouts

Average Size:

- 8-18 inches (20-46 cm.)
- 1-4 pounds (0.45-2 kg.)

Habits:

- The swifter sections of well-oxygenated streams and rivers
- A few populations are established in clear, deep ponds, especially on Cape Cod, Massachusetts

The rainbow trout, like the brown, is an import to this area. This trout was originally found on the west coast of North America, notably in California. The rainbow's high tolerance to temperature extremes and its fine sporting qualities have made this fish a favorite wherever it is found. It also responds well to hatchery life and is therefore easy to establish in favorable waters far beyond its natural range.

The Rainbow's response to the fisherman's lures is a cross between that of the brown trout and the brook trout. It is generally less selective in its feeding habits than the brown trout, and when hooked, the rainbow will give an aerial display to rival the salmon. Under proper conditions, this trout will grow to a large size in a fairly short time. It can be found in very fast-flowing parts of rivers and streams. This habit of holding in the fast water makes the rainbow an exciting fish to cast to.

Rainbows feed heavily on insects and are a favorite of fly fishermen for this reason. Small spinners and live bait will also take rainbow trout. Because of this fish's tolerance to high temperatures, it remains active in flowing water throughout the season. In still waters, the rainbow, like other inhabitants of our lakes and ponds, will retreat to deeper, cooler waters when the summer sun raises the surface water to about 60 to 65 degrees F.

Chars

Arctic Char
Salvelinus alpinus

Local Names:

- Charr
- Alpine Char
- Hudson Bay Salmon

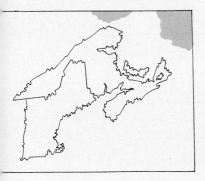

Distinguishing Characteristics:

- Similar in general appearance to the brook trout
- Caudal fin is quite deeply forked
- Color may vary widely from a uniform silvery-grey to brilliant red

Average Size:

- 18-30 inches (46-76 cm.)
- 5-10 pounds (2-5 kg.)

Habits:

- A strictly cold-water species, found in clear streams, rivers, and lakes
- Most populations have access to the sea and spend some time in the marine environment

Until recently, the Arctic char has been primarily a food fish. It forms a staple in the diet of far northern Indians and Eskimos. But with civilization's continual push into our wild lands, the Arctic char has become accessible to growing numbers of sportsmen. It is a fine game fish that puts up a fight similar to that of the brook trout. Its wilderness habitat and fine table qualities can make a fishing trip to the north woods well worth the effort. Many connoisseurs maintain that the flavor of this beautiful fish is superior to that of any salmon. A considerable commercial fishery has evolved around this fish.

167

The catch is quick frozen and shipped to restaurants all over North America. In large urban centers, char is considered a delicacy and commands a very high price.

Char will take many kinds of bait and lures, but the most common method of taking it has been spinning tackle with red and white or metallic spoons as terminal equipment. As fly fishermen expand their horizons, the Arctic char is rapidly becoming popular with those anglers fortunate enough to fish for it. Streamers and wet flies are responsible for most fly-caught Arctic char.

Many scientists consider several subspecies, including the blueback, Sunapee, and Quebec red trout, as simply being localized populations of *Salvelinus alpinus.* However, since these fishes are specifically sought by anglers in our region, they are here given special attention.

Brook Trout
Salvelinus fontinalis

Local Names:

- Squaretail
- Speckled Trout
- Brookie

Distinguishing Characteristics:

- Elongated jaws in male fish
- Vermiculated lines on back

- Orange fins with black-and-white-lined leading edges
- Bright pink, blue, and yellow spots on sides

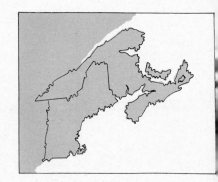

Average Size:

- 6 to 12 inches
- Occasional older specimens growing to 3 to 6 pounds

Habits:

- Cool, well-oxygenated rivers and streams
- Deep, cold lakes
- Small spring-fed ponds and flowages

The brook trout is certainly the most familiar of all the trouts found in this region. However, this fish is not really a trout. Rather, it belongs to the family known as chars. Its closest relatives are the lake trout and the Arctic char. This group also includes the rare Sunapee golden trout and the blueback trout.

Unfortunately, the brook trout requires a pure environment to maintain a self-sustaining population. Pollution and the continuing advance of civilization into the remote areas of our region have greatly reduced the number of watersheds in which this fish can maintain itself without repeated stocking.

At the turn of the last century, the entire fishery in the Rangeley Lakes of Maine was based on the brook trout. Reliable reports state that the average fish taken at that time was between six and eight pounds. Obviously, those days are long gone. Only in the wild northernmost areas of our region are there any number of such large brook trout remaining.

In searching for productive brook trout water, the angler is well advised to leave the beaten track far behind. Small ponds created by beaver dams and larger spring-fed bogs usually hold surprising numbers of trout. The spring holes in these waters will house the largest trout to be found there. Small, easily carried canoes or other watercraft are a necessity for fishing these ponds and bogs. These watersheds usually have peat bottoms and tea-colored water. These conditions are reflected in the brilliant spots and bright orange flanks of the trout. Fish taken from these isolated waters have flesh that rivals in color and flavor the best salmon steaks.

A good part of the brook trout's demise is owed to the fact that this is one of the least wary of all the trouts. This fish is an opportunist and feeds on any kind of aquatic or terrestrial insect that comes along. Larger fish feed predominately on whatever smaller fish are available, including the young of its own species. Any number of fly patterns will work at different times. Small spinning lures and that old standby, the worm, will also realize good brook trout fishing.

Brook Trout (sea-run)
Salvelinus fontinalis

Local Names:

- Sea-Trout
- Salter

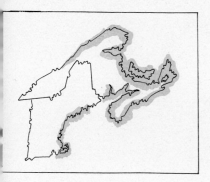

Distinguishing Characteristics:

- Differs from the freshwater races in having a distinct silvery cast over the entire body
- The head is proportionately smaller than in the freshwater fish

Average Size:

- 12-18 inches (30-46 cm.)
- 1-5 pounds (0.45-2 kg.)

Habits:

- As with all our trouts living near the sea, some brook trout enter the marine environment while others do not
- When in salt water, these fish tend to remain close to shore
- Re-enters its native rivers in the spring and early summer
- Spawns in the fall and early winter, as does the freshwater population

Until recently this beautiful fish has received little attention from sports fishermen. Even now, with interest in fishing growing very rapidly, only a very small percentage of fishermen have heard of sea-trout.

The habits and behavior of all our sea trout are very similar. Gaining size very rapidly while in the salt, these fish return to their native streams with speed and strength to spare. Runs of brook trout occur in the spring of the year. In waters where these fish occur together with Atlantic salmon, they can provide a fine bonus to the angler in search of salmon. There are many Canadian rivers where sea-trout live communally with salmon. The trout tend to ascend the rivers earlier than do the salmon, providing an early season for anglers aware of these runs.

Unlike salmon, sea trout feed throughout their freshwater run. They can be taken with a wide variety of lures. The most productive (and often the only legal) method of taking sea trout is the streamer fly or bucktail. Since the water is usually cool during the brook trout's run, sinking lines are often a necessity for best results.

As is the case with the sea-run brown trout, only a very few fishermen seek out this fish. For the angler who appreciates their fine game and table qualities, this is certainly a blessing. In fact, in waters where sea-trout are found with salmon, most salmon fishers consider the former of so little importance that it is relegated almost to the position of a nuisance.

Spawning coloration

Sunapee Trout
Salvelinus aureolus

Local Names:

- Grey Trout
- Golden Trout

Distinguishing Characteristics:

- Similar to all landlocked chars, having light spots on a solid darker ground

175

- The head is small with a pointed snout
- Caudal fin is square or slightly forked

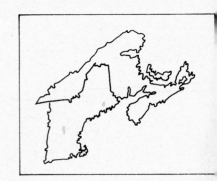

Average Size:

- 12-18 inches (30-46 cm.)
- 1-4 pounds (0.45-2 kg.)

Habits:

- The only known remaining population of pure Sunapee trout is found in Flood Pond near Ellsworth, Maine
- Habitat preference is similar to that of the lake trout

The Sunapee trout is an example of the fragility of isolated populations of fishes requiring very specific habitats. Originally recorded from Lake Sunapee in New Hampshire and later from Flood Pond in Maine, this fish has declined to its one present location. In the case of the Sunapee trout, natural circumstances seem the cause of the problem. It has been shown that Sunapee trout will cross-breed with lake trout where the two species coexist; in which case, the latter usually dominates. This situation occured in several New Hampshire lakes where plantings of pure Sunapee trout stocks were followed by the introduction of lake trout. Predation by the generally larger lake trout is also responsible for declines in Sunapee trout stocks. It can only be hoped that the one remaining population of this beautiful fish can be maintained in its pure state.

176

This char tends to keep to deeper water more than the blueback or red trout. Anglers seeking Sunapee trout are advised to use tactics proved successful for taking lake trout.

Blueback Trout

Salvelinus oquassa

Distinguishing Characteristics:

- Long, slender body
- Small head
- Deeply forked caudal fin

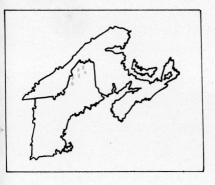

Average Size:

- 6-14 inches (15-36 cm.)
- ½-1 pound (0.22-0.45 kg.)

Habits:

- Deep, cold ponds
- Ascends streams in September or October to spawn

The history of the once extremely large population of this fish in the Rangeley Lakes region of Maine is a prime example of the delicate nature of fish populations. During the 1800s, there were reports of bushels and cartloads of bluebacks taken by net and spear while in their spawning areas. But, by the early 1900s, blueback trout were considered extinct in the Rangeley Region. This rapid decline occurred simultaneously with the introduction of the landlocked salmon in those waters, but man is certainly the despoiler of this fine isolated population. Fortunately, several other populations of this small char maintain themselves in Maine waters.

Anglers seeking this fish will find it at the surface in the spring and fall while the water is cool. During the warm months of summer, bluebacks are frequently taken by still fishing in deep water with worms as bait.

Perhaps the small size of this fish has prevented a recurrence of the Rangeley Lakes story. But intelligent management of our valuable game fishes is a necessity if there is to be any future for the sport of fishing.

Spawning coloration

Quebec
Red Trout

Salvelinus marstoni

Local Names:

- Marstone Trout

Distinguishing Characteristics:

- Flanks and fins are an intense red-orange in color

180

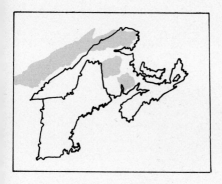

Average Size:

- 12-15 inche (31-38 cm.)
- 1-2 pounds (0.45-0.91 kg.)

Habits:

- Landlocked form of Arctic char living in clear lakes and streams of Quebec Province

The Quebec red trout, sometimes known as the Marstone trout, is found in the St. Lawrence drainage of Quebec. Its habits are similar to those of the brook trout and Arctic char. It is carnivorous and may be taken by a variety of fishing methods. All the subspecies of Arctic char tend to be smaller fish. Because of their rarity and very restricted distribution, these lovely fish must truly be considered exotics and must be carefully protected to insure their continued existence.

Lake Trout
Salvelinus namaycush

Local Names:

- Great Lakes Trout
- Mackinaw Trout
- Togue
- Laker
- Grey Trout
- Touladi

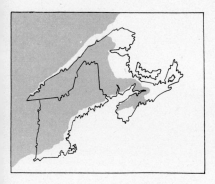

Distinguishing Characteristics:

- Large head and mouth
- Deeply forked caudal fin
- Irregular light-colored spots on a darker (brown, green, or grey) ground

Average Size:

- 14-24 inches (36-61 cm.)
- 1½-10 pounds (0.67-5 kg.)

Habits:

- Found only in deep, cold, well-oxygenated lakes
- Occasionally enters large rivers north of our range
- Usually caught around underwater ledges or shoals where it congregates to feed and spawn
- Found on or near the surface just after ice-out

For many fishermen in this region, especially those who enjoy deep trolling or ice-fishing, the lake trout is the main fishing attraction. Lake trout live remarkably long lives when compared to most other fishes. Fish from some Canadian lakes have been estimated to be 20 to 40 years of age. Lake trout often grow to great size. Specimens over ten pounds are fairly common and a few of these bottom dwellers have been recorded at the 100-pound mark.

Except in some far-northern lakes, which remain cold throughout the summer, most lake trout are caught by deep trolling live bait or artificial lures. They are taken in exactly the same manner as are landlocked salmon after their spring feeding has ended and they have gone deep. In fact, anglers fishing for one species will usually encounter the other at the same depth and temperature.

The lake trout belongs to the family of chars, which includes the brook trout, the Arctic char, and several lesser-known species. The lake trout is unusual within its group in that it depends so completely on the deep, cold waters of our lakes for its survival.

The flesh of this fish is deep pink or orange, as is the salmon's. It tends to be stronger tasting and more oily than salmon. However, many people find its flavor superior to that of any other fish.

Splake

Salvelinus fontinalis X
Salvelinus namaycush

Local Names:

- Wendigo

Distinguishing Characteristics:

- Long, slender body similar to lake trout
- Head and mouth larger than that of the brook trout, but smaller than the lake trout

185

- Caudal fin is slightly forked
- Lacks vermiculations of the brook trout's back but maintains its yellow spots
- Caudal and dorsal fins are covered with light-colored spots; these are dark in the brook trout
- Has a more rapid growth rate than either parent

Average Size:

- 15-24 inches (38-61 cm.)
- 2-10 pounds (0.91-5 kg.)

Habits:

- Shares habitat preferences of both parents, preferring deep water like the lake trout, and becoming sexually mature at an early age as in the brook trout
- Found in deep, cold, well-oxygenated lakes of Ontario and Quebec Provinces

The splake is a relative newcomer to the angling scene in our region, and fish cultural experiments with this hybrid have just begun to show promise. Few fishermen have taken one of these fish, because, to date, their distribution is limited to only a few watersheds.

Breeding experiments are underway in an attempt to develop specimens embodying the best qualities of both parents: the splake is a result of fertilizing eggs from the lake trout with sperm from the brook trout. The offspring are fertile and will reproduce under natural conditions. The diet of the splake seems less confined to bottom feeding than that of the lake trout. It subsists on aquatic insects, plankton, and leeches, as does the brook trout.

This exciting fish may well prove to be one of the most worthwhile projects undertaken by contemporary fish culturalists. Because of its parentage and environmental preferences, the splake is unlikely to disturb any habitat in which either parent fish might propagate. As improved strains of this new fish are developed, anglers in Canada and the U.S. are likely to see more and more stockings of splake in suitable waters. In any case, the history of its development will be interesting to follow.

White Fishes

Lake Whitefish
Coregonus clupeaformis

Local Names:

- Great Lakes Whitefish
- Common Whitefish
- Corigone de Lac

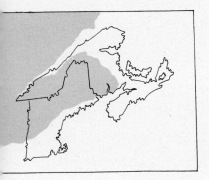

Distinguishing Characteristics:

- Closely resembles the *Salmonids* in number and placement of all fins
- Generally deeper and much more laterally compressed than the *Salmonids*
- Deeply forked caudal fin
- The snout overhangs the small mouth
- Dorsal fin is more pointed, less square than in trout and salmon
- Small pointed head

Average Size:

- 16-22 inches (41-56 cm.)
- 2-5 pounds (0.91-2 kg.)

Habits:

- Prefers/requires deep, cold lakes
- Is primarily a bottom feeder, taking a wide variety of invertebrates and small fish for sustenance
- Occasionally is found near the surface feeding on insects
- Travels in loose schools, especially when the November spawning season approaches

The lake whitefish remains the single most important commercial species in inland Canadian waters. However, stocks have declined sharply over the past two decades, due to extensive pollution of the Great Lakes watershed. Predation by the sea lamprey is also responsible for the demise of this fine food fish. However, lake whitefish continue to support a fishery that annually brings 10 to 15 million pounds to market.

Open-water anglers are not likely to be much interested in this fish, but ice fishermen take large numbers of them each winter. During the winter months, these fish are usually found at the same levels as the trout or salmon with which they often mingle. They can be taken by using live minnows or smelt for bait. Small jigs and fly-jigs will also bring strikes. The whitefish have mouths that are much softer than those of salmon or trout and must be carefully played to prevent pulling the hook out.

Where whitefish and lake trout are found together, the smaller whitefish is consumed in large numbers by the lake trout.

Many people believe the whitefish to be the best possible table fare.

Round Whitefish

Prosopium cylindraceum

Local Names:

- Pilot Fish
- Frost Fish
- Round Fish
- Menominee
- Minomini Round

Distinguishing Characteristics:

- Body is of a slender, elongated, cigar shape
- Nearly round in cross section
- Small, pointed head and mouth
- Deeply forked caudal fin

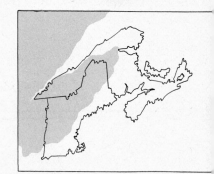

Average Size:

- 12-15 inches (31-38 cm.)
- ¾-1 pound (0.33-0.45 kg.)

Habits:

- Primarily a fish of large rivers
- Inhabits deep, cold lakes in our region
- Generally remains in relatively shallow water

The importance of this fish as game is minor. It is taken occasionally by anglers, usually while they are fishing for other species. It is frequently found coexisting with trout and salmon. It is actively sought by anglers in the northeastern part of New Brunswick, but its usual reluctance to take a hook puts it rather low on fishermen's lists.

Like the other members of its family, the round whitefish is an excellent flavored fish. It generally reaches the table through the commercial market. In the area of the Great Lakes, the round whitefish supports a small but active commercial fishery.

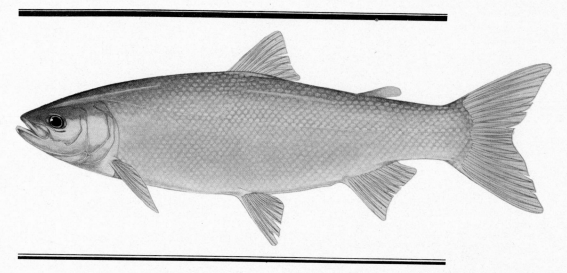

Cisco

Coregonus artedii

Local Names:

- Grayback
- Blueback
- Lake Herring
- Tullibu
- Haring de Lac

194

Distinguishing Characteristics:

- Very similar to the lake whitefish
- Has a more cigar-shaped body than *C. clupeaformis*
- The mouth is at the frontmost extremity of the head and is not overhung by the snout

Average Size:

- 8-14 inches (20-36 cm.)
- 1-1½ pounds (0.45-0.67 kg.)

Habits:

- Found feeding at the surface when the water is cool in spring and fall
- Travels in schools
- Seeks deeper, cooler water in summer

The cisco is sought by anglers not because of its game quality, but rather because it is an exceptionally fine-tasting fish.

Cisco are taken in the spring and fall when they feed heavily on insects emerging at the surface. They may be taken at this time by using small dry flies or streamers or small flashing spinners.

Like the lake whitefish, the shallow-water cisco has for many years been

195

the basis of an extensive commercial fishery in Canada, where it is most abundant. However, pollution and predation by the sea lamprey have caused a continuing decline in that once-vast fishery.

The Pikes

Muskellunge

Esox masquinongy

Local Names:

- Muskie
- Maskinonge
- Lunge
- Tiger Muskellunge

Distinguishing Characteristics:

- Very large average size

- Has no scales on lower half of cheeks and operculum
- Has 12-18 pores on the underside of lower jaw

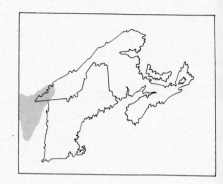

Average Size:

- 24-48 inches (60-120 cm.)
- 5-36 pounds (2-16 kg.)

Habits:

- Solitary, usually remaining in one jealously defended area for several months
- Feeds almost entirely on smaller fishes but will devour young waterfowl, snakes, and land mammals that may enter the water
- May cross-breed with northern pike under natural conditions

The muskellunge, occupying a much smaller range than the northern pike, is probably sought by just as many anglers as the pike. Its following is made up of a coterie of very devoted fishermen who spend many often fruitless hours in pursuit of this giant of our freshwater fishes.

This fish is found in some very beautiful watersheds; this, combined with its wariness and stong, spectacular fight is responsible for the muskellunge's popularity as a game fish. Most anglers prefer to cover large areas of "good looking" water by slowly trolling a large swimming plug or bait fish behind a slow-moving boat. Casting plugs or bait often produces good catches (which may consist of one or two fish per week) of muskellunge. The idea that one may be just as likely to hook a 30- or 40-pound fish as easily as a 5-pounder is a large part of the "magic" often associated with this type of fishing.

At one time *E. masquinongy* supported a fairly substantial commercial fishery in Canada. But, as the fish gained in popularity with anglers, government officials became aware that this great fish was worth more to the economy as a game fish. For that reason strictly enforced bag limits and seasons have been established to protect the muskellunge. Because this protection insures consistent stocks of fish, sporting camps, guides, and outfitters continue to realize a good profit by providing services to visiting and resident anglers in search of this species.

Unlike its smaller cousin, the northern pike, the muskellunge is widely esteemed as a food fish. When skinned, to remove the heavy layer of mucus, it provides fine, white, flaky meat. It is usually baked, poached, or steaked for broiling or frying.

Northern Pike
Esox lucius

Local Names:

- Great Northern Pike
- Jack
- Jackfish
- Snake
- Grand Brochet

Distinguishing Characteristics:

- Cheek and upper half of gill cover are scaled
- Long, slender body with cream-colored irregular spots on a dark ground

200

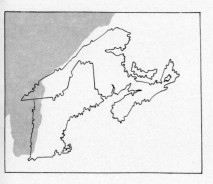

- Deeply forked caudal fin
- Dorsal and anal fins are set far back on the body
- Very long "duck bill"-shaped head
- Mouth filled with many very sharp teeth
- Bottom of lower jaw has ten sensory pores or holes

Average Size:

- 18-36 inches (46-91 cm.)
- 2-10 pounds (0.91-5 kg.)

Habits:

- Inhabits shallow, weedy areas of lakes, ponds, and rivers
- Spends most of its time hanging motionless within the shelter of weeds or other protective objects
- Usually takes its prey (and the angler's lures) in a sudden, very rapid rush

Much more a game fish than a commercial species, the northern pike will put on a spectacular show of rapid leaps and long runs when hooked. Pike fishing generates a great deal of excitement, since the fisherman never knows when he casts a lure or bait if the strike will come from a small or a very large pike.

The methods most often used in pike fishing are spinning or bait casting with plugs or metal spoons as lures. The angler will move slowly along the edges of weed beds or submerged brush or log piles. Each likely looking spot requires a well-placed cast. Most often, when a pike takes, it will do so in a very rapid rush. When hooked the pike makes every effort to re-enter the shelter of its favorite weed bed. In an attempt to free itself from the hook, a pike will often leap clear of the water in "tail-walking" or somersaulting jumps.

There are times when uncooperative pike can be enticed to strike only by slowly trolling a plug or spoon in deeper water or along underwater ledges and shoals. When a lure is retrieved it will sometimes be followed very close to shore or to the boat by a pike that is curious but not wholly convinced of the bait's authenticity. A large pike following in this manner is likely to cause any angler to hold his breath and hope for the best.

An on-going debate continues among anglers concerning the pike's merits as a game and food fish. Some would have this fish banned from all waters and tables, while others like nothing better than the fight and taste of a good northern pike.

In recent years, this fish has been pursued by fly fishermen whose light tackle approach makes it a superb quarry for the angler using the "long wand" and a steel leader.

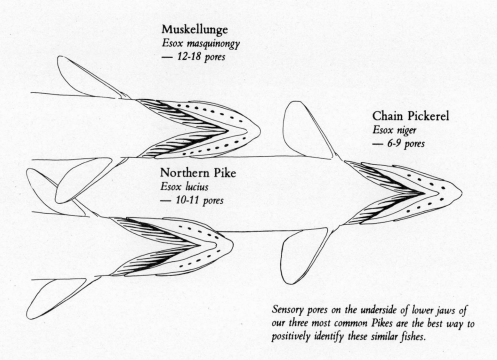

Muskellunge
Esox masquinongy
— *12-18 pores*

Chain Pickerel
Esox niger
— *6-9 pores*

Northern Pike
Esox lucius
— *10-11 pores*

Sensory pores on the underside of lower jaws of our three most common Pikes are the best way to positively identify these similar fishes.

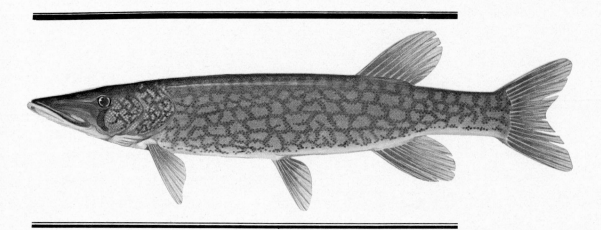

Chain Pickerel

Esox niger

Local Names:

- Pickerel
- Eastern Pickerel
- Grass Pickerel
- Picquerelle
- Brochet Maille

Distinguishing Characteristics:

- The cheeks and gill covers are completely scaled
- Has only 6-9 sensory pores on underside of lower jaw

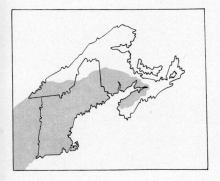

- Distinct dark-colored chain pattern on a lighter ground
- Dark vertical bar running downward over cheek from the lower margin of the eye

Average Size:

- 15-26 inches (38-66 cm.)
- 1-4 pounds (0.45-2 kg.)

Habits:

- Favors shallow weed beds of grasses or water lillies
- Will hold in shallow water close to any type of sheltering protrusion
- Takes a very wide variety of foods, including snakes, frogs, and even mice when available

Within our range, the chain pickerel is the most widely distributed member of the pike family. In Canadian waters it is usually taken by anglers in search of other species. However, in New England, the pickerel is often sought by light-tackle sportsmen. It forms the base of a rather extensive winter ice-fishery, with the average catch 15 to 18 inches (38 to 46 cm.) in length and one to two pounds in weight. It is taken largely as a food fish, and its flesh, although bony, if properly prepared, makes fine eating.

Chain pickerel are hard fighters, making up what they lack in size by providing the angler an acrobatic display and strong runs similar to those of the northern pike. As with so many of our game fishes, the chain pickerel is rapidly gaining favor with fly fishermen. A trout-sized fly-fishing outfit, some bright streamer flies, and surface poppers can afford the avid fly fisherman many hours of fine sport, usually quite close to home.

The most common open water method used for pickerel fishing is spinning or bait casting with surface or shallow-running weedless lures. Morning and evening are the best times to take pickerel, but these hungry predators may be taken throughout the day, especially during their spring spawning activity.

Grass Pickerel

Esox vermiculatus

Local Names:

- Mud Pickerel
- Little Pickerel
- Brochat Vermicule

Distinguishing Characteristics:

- The smallest member of the pike family
- Strongly resembles the northern pike

207

- Cheeks and gill covers are fully scaled
- Can be distinguished from pike and muskellunge by its dark vermiculated bars or spots on the sides

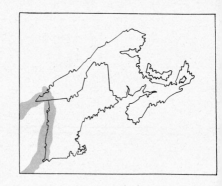

Average Size:

- 6-10 inches (15-25 cm.)
- ½ pound (0.22 kg.)

Habits:

- Frequents weed beds and submerged brush
- Often found in isolated pools of rivers and streams during low-water conditions

This fish is, because of its size and limited distribution, not usually considered a game fish. It is included here because it is often confused with the young of northern pike or muskellunge.

Redfin Pickerel

Esox Americanus

Local Names:

- Grass Pickerel
- Bulldog Pickerel
- Banded Pickerel
- Red-finned Pike
- Brochet d'Amérique

Distinguishing Characteristics:

- Long body, cylindrical in cross-section
- Both the cheek and operculum are completely scaled

- The dark bar emanating from the lower margin of the eye slants backward at a more distinct angle than in the grass pickerel

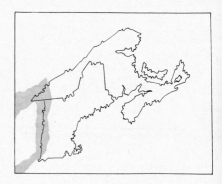

Average Size:

- 6-12 inches (15-31 cm.)
- ½ pound (0.22 kg.)

Habits:

- Slow, weed-filled streams
- Found less frequently than other members of the pike family in ponds and shallow weedy portions of larger lakes

Like its cousin the grass pickerel, this small predator is not usually sought by anglers. It is most likely to be taken by fishermen seeking bass or crappies and is often confused with the young of the northern pike. Like all the members of this clan, this little pickerel is a voracious feeder and will sometimes strike lures that are nearly as long as itself. It is not large enough to be of much value as a food fish.

Perches

Yellow Perch

Perca flavescens

Local Names:

- Perch
- Lake Perch
- American Perch
- Red Perch
- Perchaude

Distinguishing Characteristics:

- Six or seven wide, dark vertical bars on sides
- Ventral fins are usually bright orange
- Dorsal fins are separate
- First dorsal has strong, sharp spines

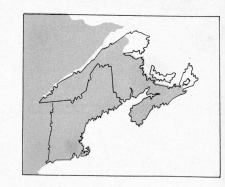

Average Size:

- 6-12 inches (15-31 cm.)
- ½-1½ pounds (0.22-0.67 kg.)

Habits:

- Usually found in large schools but may be solitary or in small groups
- Found in shallow waters of lakes, ponds, and quiet streams and rivers

Generally running quite small, the yellow perch is considered by many to be merely a "kids' fish." Indeed, many young anglers have spent many enjoyable hours "dunking worms" in the hopes of taking yellow perch.

In addition to being a fine flavored pan fish, the yellow perch serves as a forage fish for larger game species. It does, however, tend to overpopulate and become a nuisance.

The yellow perch has for many years been an important part of the Great Lakes commercial fishery. In fact, it is probably the first fish to have been exploited by this inland fishing fleet. Each year, many thousands of yellow perch reach the commercial market. They are sometimes sold fresh and are often processed into fish cakes and the like. The yellow perch maintains a large and faithful following of ice fishermen who like nothing better than a winter fish fry.

Walleye
Stizostedion vitreum

Local Names:

- Pickerel
- Pike Perch
- Walleye Pike
- Walleyed Pickerel
- Doré

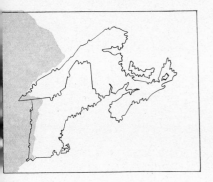

Distinguishing Characteristics:

- There were, until recently, two subspecies of this fish — blue walleye, *S. vitreum glaucum,* and yellow walleye, *S. vitreum vitreum,* which differ primarily in color, rate of growth, and spawning time
- Long, deep head with large mouth; jaws are equal length
- Upper jawbone (maxillary) extends to the rear edge of the eye
- Jaws contain large, strong teeth

Average Size:

- 15-24 inches (38-61 cm.)
- 2-5 pounds (0.91-2 kg.)

Habits:

- Found in lakes and large rivers
- Often ascends tributary streams to spawn in the spring of the year
- Usually taken from shallow water but will seek deep, cooler water if surface temperatures rise very high

Avidly sought by both sport and commercial fishermen, the walleye is one of the most valuable species found in the inland waters of Canada. There were, until recently, two subspecies of this fish, but the blue walleye is now considered extinct or very rare in all of its original range. The two subspecies differ only slightly. The blue walleye has a distinct blue-grey cast to its body and is more distinctly marked with dark irregular bars generally above the lateral line. The yellow walleye grows larger and at a faster rate than the blue.

The catch of walleye from Ontario waters has averaged around four million pounds in recent years; this does not include fish taken by anglers. It ranks third in commercial importance after perch and smelt.

The walleye is usually taken by anglers still fishing with live minnows as bait. Spinning lures such as spoons and spinners are also responsible for a large number of walleyes. Ice fishing is a very popular method for taking this fish. Walleyes are not spectacular fighters but are very strong, and when hooked will struggle constantly to reach the bottom or other shelter. As reflected by the economic importance of this fish, it provides fine table fare.

Sauger
Stizostedion canadense

Local Names:

- Eastern Sauger
- Sand Pike
- Sand Pickerel
- Doré Noir

217

Distinguishing Characteristics:

- More slender throughout its length than the similar walleye
- May be distinguished from the walleye in that it has two or three rows of dark spots on the first (spiny) dorsal fin
- Cheeks are covered with rough scales
- Body is distinctly marked by dark, irregular blotches

Average Size:

- 12-15 inches (31-38 cm.)
- 1-2 pounds (0.45-0.91 kg.)

Habits:

- Inhabits lakes and larger slow-moving rivers
- Is generally found near the bottom feeding on fishes and aquatic nymphs
- Often found in turbid or silted waters

The sauger, because of its smaller average size and more restricted range, is not generally as popular as a game fish as its cousin, the walleye. In fact sauger are usually taken by anglers seeking other species. Because of its preference for turbid or silty waters, this smaller fish can provide sport where the walleye is absent.

Sauger are primarily bottom feeders, except when they move into shallow water at night. They will take a variety of baits and lures, showing a preference for live minnows and jigs. Still fishing or slow trolling are the methods most commonly employed by sauger fishermen.

Like the walleye, the sauger is an excellent table fish, having white, firm, flaky flesh.

Sunfishes

Bluegill
Lepomis macrochirus

Local Names:

- Blue Sunfish
- Sunfish

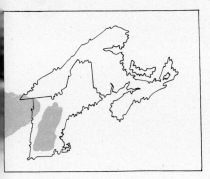

- Bream
- Roach
- Crapet Arlequin

Distinguishing Characteristics:

- Very deep, laterally compressed body
- Steep forehead
- Small mouth with upper jaw ending at the front margin of the eye
- Distinct deep blue or black flap on upper rear margin of gill cover

Average Size:

- 7-10 inches (18-25 cm.)
- ½-1 pound (0.22-0.45 kg.)

Habits:

- Usually found in warm, shallow, weed-filled ponds and slow streams
- Occurs in nearly any available type of water
- Most often found near shore at depths varying from just below the surface to 15-20 feet

The bluegill and its close relative, the pumpkinseed, are easily the best known and most easily observed of our freshwater fishes. These are very active,

221

inquisitive fish whose curiosity brings them swimming quickly toward any commotion in or on the nearby water. Almost everyone who has ever "wet a line" has caught one of these very game miniatures. When caught on light tackle, the bluegill puts up a strong, rod-bending fight. It will generally strike hard, and when it feels the hook will make a series of fast, short runs punctuated by swimming in large circles with its flat sides serving as a plane.

It goes without saying that this is a fine game fish when given the advantage of light tackle and line. Although its flesh is somewhat bony, it has a fine, sweet flavor.

Pumpkinseed

Lepomis gibbosus

Local Names:

- Sunfish
- Yellow Sunfish
- Sunny
- Kibbie

- Sun Bass
- Crapet-Soleil

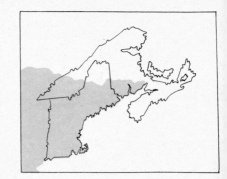

Distinguishing Characteristics:

- The rear margin of the flap on the gill cover has a distinct red spot in addition to a dark blue or black mark, which is generally larger than the red
- Very deep, laterally compressed body with a high, steep forehead
- Moderately forked caudal fin
- Usually a dark spot on the rear lower margin of the soft second dorsal or the back in the same area
- Very small mouth with short maxillary
- Several wavy blue or emerald lines radiating back from the snout and eye

Average Size:

- 6-9 inches (15-23 cm.)
- ½-¾ pound (0.22-0.33 kg.)

Habits:

- Generally found in warm, shallow, weedy ponds, lakes, or slow streams

- Occasionally found in nearly all water types where it may or may not thrive
- Spawns in late spring after the female has prepared a shallow circular nest with a coarse gravel bottom; the male jealously defends the nest
- Usually found near shore in shallow water

Within our range, this is by far the most common member of the prolific sunfish family. It occurs in some very unexpected and untypical habitats, including the quieter portions of some of our best trout streams. It is readily available and willing to provide fine sport throughout the open-water season. In favorable habitats, the pumpkinseed will attain relatively large sizes. A 10- to 12-inch specimen, weighing in the neighborhood of one pound, can give any angler some very pleasant moments.

The pumpkinseed will take nearly any type of natural bait or artificial lure or fly. It is probably most commonly caught by fishermen using worms for bait, but many fly-fishing enthusiasts avidly seek this brightly colored fish. It will take any kind of fly but is particularly fond of very small popping or sliding bugs fished around weed beds.

Large pumpkinseeds are sometimes eaten. Their flesh is firm and sweet but considered too bony by many.

Redbreast Sunfish
Lepomis auritus

Local Names:

- Yellowbelly Sunfish
- Redbelly
- Longear Sunfish
- Crapet Rouge

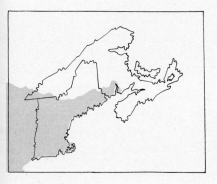

Distinguishing Characteristics:

- The entire earflap is dark blue or black
- The belly is usually a bright red or orange in color
- Very similar to the pumpkinseed

Average Size:

- 5-7 inches (13-18 cm.)
- ½-¾ pound (0.22-0.33 kg.)

Habits:

- Generally occurs in ponds, lakes, and slow-moving streams
- Often found inhabiting the same waters as the closely related bluegill and pumpkinseed sunfish

All that applies to the pumpkinseed sunfish holds true for the redbreast as well. It inhabits the same type of water and is just as willing to take any bait or small artificial lure that comes within its reach. Its range is almost as extensive as that of the pumpkinseed's, and the two species are often taken from the same waters. Both the redbreast and the pumpkinseed are usually relegated to the department of "kid's fish," but both provide fine sport when caught on light tackle.

Small specimens of the sunfish tribe make fine aquarium fish, as they are very hardy and will feed actively on many types of food.

227

Rock Bass

Ambloplites rupestris

Local Names:

- Redeye Bass
- Goggle-eye
- Northern Rock Bass
- Rock Sunfish
- Crapet de Rocke

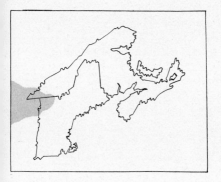

Distinguishing Characteristics:

- Body is not nearly as high from dorsal to ventral as in the other sunfishes
- Very large, red eye
- Large mouth with maxillary extending to the mid-point of the eye
- Lower jaw projects slightly beyond upper

Average Size:

- 6-10 inches (15-26 cm.)
- ½-¾ pound (0.22-0.33 kg.)

Habits:

- Occurs most commonly in shallow, rocky areas of clear, cool lakes and ponds
- May be found in the lower reaches of larger streams
- Often shares its habitat with the smallmouth bass

The rock bass is a small but scrappy sunfish that prefers a habitat nearly identical to that favored by the smallmouth bass. The rock bass shares with the rest of its clan a willingness to devour whatever bait or lure the angler might offer. When a rock bass takes the offering, it does so with a force that often leads the fisherman to believe that a much larger fish has taken the hook.

As the battle progresses, the rock bass provides a fight that, pound for pound, matches much larger species.

Because it does not grow very large, the rock bass is often overlooked as a food fish, but it is equal to any of the other sunfishes in flavor.

Black Crappie

Pomoxis nigromaculatus

Local Names:

- Crappie
- Speckled Bass
- Calico Bass
- Oswego Bass
- Marigane Noire

231

Distinguishing Characteristics:

- Body is extremely laterally compressed
- Less deep from dorsal to ventral than the other sunfishes
- Has a large eye and mouth, with maxillary extending to the rear margin of the eye

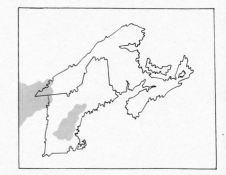

Average Size:

- 7-12 inches (18-31 cm.)
- ½-1 pound (0.22-0.45 kg.)

Habits:

- Frequents shallow, often weedy areas of lakes, ponds, and rivers
- A warm-water species not often found in deep, cold lakes
- Usually travels in loose schools
- Seldom found far from the shoreline

This attractive member of the sunfish family averages larger than its cousins, but shares their preference for the weed-filled areas of ponds, lakes, and slow-moving streams.

The black crappie is an ideal quarry for the ultra-light tackle enthusiast. It is very fond of smaller streamer and wet flies as well as smaller spinning lures and tiny jigs. The bait fishermen in pursuit of this fish will usually use a small, live minnow hooked through the back as bait. The crappie has a softer mouth than is common to the rest of its tribe and must be handled accordingly. "Horsing the fish in" will often result in the fisherman tearing the hook out of the fish's mouth. The crappie is a strong, circling fighter that will test any light-tackle angler's skill. Where it is common, this attractive fish is a favorite with fly fishermen.

Black Basses

Smallmouth Bass
Micropterus dolomieui

Local Names:

- Black Bass
- Smallmouth
- Bronzeback
- Achigan à Petite Bouche

234

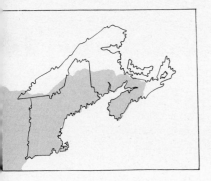

Distinguishing Characteristics:

- Margin of upper jaw (maxillary) never extends beyond the rear edge of the eye
- Usually marked with 10-15 darker vertical bars on a bronze or green-bronze ground
- The cheeks and gill covers are marked by several dark diagonal bars radiating outward and backward from the snout
- Overall body shape is deep and robust

Average Size:

- 12-18 inches (31-46 cm.)
- 1½-4 pounds (0.67-2 kg.)

Habits:

- Found in lakes, clear ponds, and rivers; sometimes taken in rather swift water
- A fish of shallow water, seldom taken below the 20-foot mark, even in summer
- Feeds on any available organism, including insects, crayfish, frogs, and small fishes
- Spawns in late May and early June — males are very protective of nests and eggs, and can be easily enticed to strike at this time of year
- Usually found over gravel bottoms with large boulders for cover

235

Inhabiting a wide range of environments, the smallmouth bass provides sport for a great many anglers in our region. Its habitat preference runs to clear, cool, well-oxygenated waters; it is often found communally with landlocked salmon and lake trout, especially in Maine.

This active fish is also found in many clear-running streams and rivers, where it often competes with our trouts for cover and food. In some cases, introduction of smallmouth bass has resulted in a sharp decline in trout populations.

The smallmouth bass is a game fish of excellent quality; its hefty size, seemingly boundless strength, and fine flavor make it a much-sought species. Fortunately, it is a prolific spawner and seems to have little or no trouble sustaining large, healthy populations.

Smallmouths begin to feed heavily as soon as the water has warmed into the 60s F (10-15° C). They will take almost any properly presented bait, lure, or fly as the mood strikes them; yet these are very moody fish. One day of spectacular smallmouth fishing may be followed by one in which few if any fish can be enticed. Surface lures (including flies) are favorites, since they make the whole experience of taking the fish more visible. Smallmouth bass will usually strike with a strong, decisive rush, stripping off large amounts of line before ending the first run, often by clearing the water in a frantic leap. A good-sized fish will often jump five or six times before tiring. Its runs are strong and often difficult to control.

Eastern Maine, with its many large, cool, clear lakes, has long been a mecca for sportsmen seeking this fish.

Fly fishermen are becoming increasingly interested in the smallmouth bass. Surface poppers, streamer flies, and even dry flies will take these fine fish. A day of taking strong, hefty, wild fish can provide a much needed tonic for the fisherman used to catching small hatchery-reared trout on overcrowded streams. But the smallmouth can be just as selective as a quarry as any trout and is now beginning to take its rightful place among the favorites of the fly-fishing fraternity.

Largemouth Bass, *Micropterus salmoides*

Smallmouth Bass, *Micropterus dolomieui*

Deep notch between first and second dorsal fins

Caudal fin is only slightly forked; often rounded in old specimens

Single dark band runs the length of the body; this tends to fade with age

Upper jaw, maxillary, extends beyond rear margin of the eye

Notch between dorsal fins is not as deep as in Largemouth

Caudal fin is moderately forked

Dark broken stripes run vertically on a lighter ground

Upper jaw, maxillary, ends near midpoint of the eye

Comparison of Largemouth and Small-mouth Bass

Largemouth Bass
Micropterus salmoides

Local Names:

- Black Bass
- Largemouth
- Green Bass
- Achigan à Grande Bouche

238

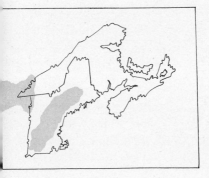

Distinguishing Characteristics:

- Large head and mouth; deep, robust body
- Upper jawbone (maxillary) extends well beyond the rear margin of the eye
- In young fish a single dark, broken stripe runs the entire length of the body. This often disappears with age
- Caudal fin is more deeply forked than in the smallmouth bass

Average Size:

- 14-18 inches (36-46 cm.)
- 2-4 pounds (0.91-2 kg.)

Habits:

- A fish of warm, shallow waters
- Often found in weed beds or near stumps or other outcroppings
- Seldom descends below the 20-30 foot (6.10-9.15 m.) level
- Prefers warmer, often less clear, water than does the smallmouth bass
- Spawns in May and June, with males guarding the nest and the newborn young

The largemouth bass occupies less of our range than does the smallmouth. In fact, its center of abundance and most productive waters lies well to the south of New England. But, through introduction, adaptability, and stamina, the largemouth bass continues to increase its range.

Bass fishermen have long engaged in arguments that attempt to determine which of the two species is the superior game fish. In our region sheer numbers and availability give the smallmouth a decided advantage. But a day of fishing for largemouth bass will provide just as much excitement as can be found in taking any of our freshwater species.

Largemouth bass often share their habitat with chain pickerel and smaller pan fishes, such as sunfish and perch. Unless the angler confines himself to the use of large bass lures, he is likely to take a mixed bag of warm-water fish while casting for largemouth bass.

The same lures and baits used for taking smallmouth bass will usually produce good largemouth catches as well, but, because of its larger mouth and predatory habits, this fish is more willing to devour larger, less delicate offerings than its cousin. Like the smallmouth, the largemouth is a very unpredictable quarry. It may be found in great numbers in shallow water, almost on shore; and a week later, the same water will produce little or no action. When a good largemouth is hooked, it will put up a battle very similar to that of the smallmouth. But, while the smallmouth tends to "cartwheel" its way out of the water, the largemouth frequently "tail walks" along the surface. The author makes no judgment concerning which of these acrobatic maneuvers is the more heart-stopping. Since this fish usually inhabits waters where many bottom obstructions are found, it will usually try to regain its cover when hooked. Any angler, using appropriate tackle, will find himself and his equipment put to a challenging test each time a good fish takes the hook. Many largemouths are lost every year when they manage to hopelessly entangle the fisherman's line.

Another debate also continues regarding the relative flavor of smallmouth versus largemouth. The slight advantage goes again to the smallmouth, only because the muddy bottoms that the largemouth so often prefers may give its flesh an unsavory taste.

Suckers

Shorthead Redhorse
Maxostoma macrolepidotum

Local Names:

- Northern Redhorse
- Common Redhorse
- Common Mullet
- Red Sucker
- Suceur Rouge

242

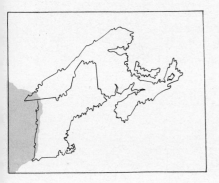

Distinguishing Characteristics:

- Moderately laterally compressed body
- Profile of back has a moderately high arch, which peaks at the leading edge of the single, soft dorsal fin
- Caudal fin is deeply forked
- No scales on head
- Small inferior mouth is overhung by snout
- Large anal fin

Average Size:

- 12-18 inches (31-46 cm.)
- 1-3 pounds (0.45-2 kg.)

Habits:

- Inhabits large, deep lakes and ponds
- A bottom feeder, taking its food by probing the ground while sucking in edible matter
- Ascends rivers and streams to spawn

This fish is restricted to the westernmost part of our range. Even at its center of abundance, this redhorse is not very common.

As is the case with our more abundant suckers, this fish is taken in some numbers when it enters streams and rivers to spawn. It will provide a good fight when hooked, partly because of its large average size. Its flesh is white, firm, and flaky but filled with small bones.

Quillback

Carpiodes cyprinus

Local Names:

- Quillback Carpsucker
- Eastern Carpsucker
- Quillback Sucker

- Silver Carp
- Mullet
- Couette

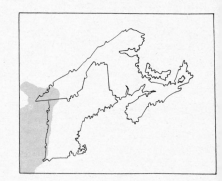

Distinguishing Characteristics:

- Very deep bodied with maximum depth at leading edge of dorsal fin
- Strongly laterally compressed
- Leading edge of dorsal is extended into a long, thin edge
- No scales on head
- Caudal fin is deeply forked
- Small sucker mouth
- Large, coarse scales

Average Size:

- 10-15 inches (25-38 cm.)
- 2-5 pounds (0.91-2 kg.)

Habits:

- A bottom feeder occurring in lakes, ponds, and large rivers
- Ascends streams (where available) to spawn
- Will spawn in flooded areas in shallow portions of lakes or larger rivers

246

Like the redhorse, this fish is of only minor importance (especially within our range) to man. It is generally taken by anglers seeking other lake dwelling species. It will take nearly any small bait made from animal matter.

The quillback provides fair sport when taken on light or ultra-light tackle. It probably contributes in some minor way to the commercial fishery of the Great Lakes region.

Local Names:

- Sucker
- Common White Sucker
- Black Sucker
- Meunier Noir

Distinguishing Characteristics:

- Elongate, robust body, oval in cross section
- Inferior mouth, overhung by snout

White Sucker

Catostomus commersoni

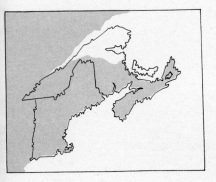

- Large, coarse scales, crowded toward the head
- Large, strong fins

Average Size:

- 12-18 inches (31-46 cm.)
- 1-3 pounds (0.45-2 kg.)

Habits:

- Found throughout our range in lakes, ponds, rivers and streams
- Usually found on or near the bottom in relatively shallow water where it probes the ground for food
- Often travels in schools
- Spawns in the spring, usually in rivers and streams, occasionally over shallow sand or gravel beds of the lakes

The white sucker maintains a debatable status as a game fish even in waters where trout, salmon, and bass are common. During the spring spawning runs, suckers swarm up streams where many are taken by fishermen using spears. A hook baited with worms and sunk to the bottom will also attract this fish. When taken on light tackle, the white sucker provides fine sport which is increased by its generally fair size.

The flesh of this fish is sweet but very bony.

Minnows

Carp
Cyprinus carpio

Local Names:

- German Carp
- European Carp
- Leather Carp
- Carpe

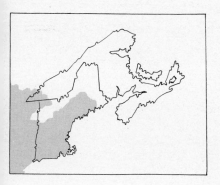

Distinguishing Characteristics:

- Has a deep, heavy body,which is slightly laterally compressed
- One long continuous soft rayed dorsal fin
- Deeply forked caudal fin
- Large scales
- Small, terminal mouth slightly overhung by snout
- A short barbel on each side at the corner of the mouth

Average Size:

- 12-24 inches (31-61 cm.)
- 5-15 pounds (2-7 kg.)

Habits:

- Feeds on bottom by rooting in mud
- Feeds on aquatic vegetation and small organisms
- Inhabits warm, shallow ponds and larger rivers
- A very adaptable fish which has been responsible for destroying the habitat of more desirable game fishes by killing vegetation and muddying the water

A native of Asia the carp was introduced into North American waters in the early to mid 1800s. Because it is a very hardy and adaptable fish, its range has greatly increased since its introduction. The carp was introduced on its merits as a food fish. It grows rapidly and is easily reared and cultivated in captivity.

Unfortunately this fish competes very successfully with other fishes, especially the warm-water game species such as bass and pike. Its habit of grubbing or rooting in the softer areas of a pond, lake, or river bottom raises mud and silt which deprive the water of oxygen needed by more prized game fishes. For this reason laws prohibiting the use of carp as bait have been passed throughout our region.

For most sportsmen this fish has been and is still considered nothing but trash. But in recent years, many bow hunters have converted their archery equipment to bow-fishing rigs by adding a spool or reel or line. This aspect of the sport amounts to something like spear-fishing above the surface of the water.

For the rod and reel enthusiast, a small hook embedded in a doughball, potato cube, or small worm can lead to a long battle with a strong, untiring fish. Because of its large size and great endurance, the carp can provide fine sport on light tackle.

The carp maintains a European reputation as a fine food fish. In North America, especially where trout, salmon or bass are available, the carp is almost unanimously regarded as less than edible. But, with proper preparation this fish can provide a fine meal.

Golden Shiner
Notemigonus crysoleucas

Local Names:

- Shiner
- Roach
- Pond Shiner
- Bream
- Chatte de L'est

Distinguishing Characteristics:

- Small, pointed head with a small, terminal mouth
- Single dorsal fin set well back on the rather highly arched back
- Body is strongly laterally compressed
- Lateral line curves far down on the body
- Forked caudal fin has rounded lobes

Average Size:

- 4-8 inches (10-20 cm.)
- 4-8 ounces (113-226 g.)

Habits:

- Found in warm, still or slow moving waters
- Prefers weed filled areas over a soft bottom
- Usually encountered only in shallow areas

Depending upon the age of the angler questioned, the golden shiner's claim to game fish status varies widely. These small but rather attractive minnows are largely responsible for launching many youngsters into the sport of fishing.

Where it occurs, the golden shiner generally abounds; and since it travels in loose schools, it can provide hours of fun for the young sportsman.

As a bait fish, the golden shiner dominates the market in our region. It is very hardy, easy to rear in captivity, and able to withstand a wide range of temperatures. Since it is native to many of the waters where it is used as bait, it is readily accepted as food by the resident game fishes. While filling this ecological niche as forage and bait-fish, the golden shiner contributes a great deal to the sport fishing industry.

Fallfish

Semotilus corporalis

Local Names:

- Chub
- Stone Roller
- Lake Chub
- American Chub
- Ouitouche

256

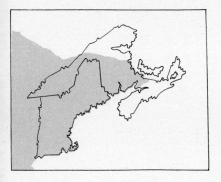

Distinguishing Characteristics:

- The body is more robust than in most other minnows
- A large, rounded head with moderate size terminal mouth
- Single dorsal fin emanates from about the mid point of the back

Average Size:

- 6-12 inches (15-31 cm.)
- ½-1 pound (0.22-0.45 kg.)

Habits:

- Occurs in nearly all types of fresh water within our range
- Usually found in open water but occasionally taken near weeds
- Frequently encountered in large schools comprised of individuals of various ages

The fallfish, usually called a chub in our region, is most often used as a bait fish; especially as cut-bait. As live bait, it is very hardy and can withstand a wide range of temperatures.

Populations of fallfish thrive in a remarkably wide variety of habitats. One would think that, as a member of the minnow family, it would be restricted to life in warmer water. But, in fact, anglers most often encounter this fish while fishing for trout in swift, clear streams. When taken in this

257

manner, it is usually considered no more than a nuisance. However, when the trout fishing is slow, the fallfish can provide a willing subject for experimentation by the angler. The fallfish is a voracious feeder and will devour any form of bait or artificial fly or lure. Larger specimens (in the 12- to 15-inch class) are strong fighters, often being mistaken for trout. Fallfish are not usually used as table fish, as their flesh is filled with many small bones.

Creek Chub

Semotilus atromaculatus

Local Names:

- Chub
- Horned Chub
- Horned Dace
- Brook Chub
- Mulet à Cornes

Distinguishing Characteristics:

- Very similar in appearance to the fallfish
- Black spot on lower leading edge of single soft dorsal fin
- Large, terminal mouth with maxillary extending to mid point of the eye
- Young specimens have a dark band running along the middle of each side from snout to tail

Average Size:

- 4-8 inches (10-20 cm.)
- ¼-½ pound (0.11-0.22 kg.)

Habits:

- Found almost exclusively in small brooks and streams
- Seldom found in lakes and ponds

This small fish is not truly a game fish except when taken incidentally by anglers fishing for other species (usually trout). It is, however, very frequently used as bait, and larger specimens can be easily confused with its close relative, the fallfish.

In its natural habitat, which consists primarily of streams shared with trout, it provides good forage for the larger game fish.

260

Mooneye

Hiodon tergisus

Local Names:

- River Whitefish
- Freshwater Herring
- Toothed Herring
- Laquaiche Argentée

Distinguishing Characteristics:

- Strongly laterally compressed deep body
- Large scales

261

- Small head and small terminal mouth
- Large, round eye
- Single soft rayed dorsal emanates well back on the body
- Deeply forked caudal fin

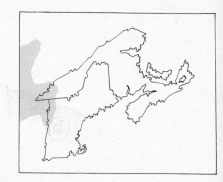

Average Size:

- 8–12 inches (21–31 cm.)
- ½–¾ pound (0.22–0.56 kg.)

Habits:

- A fish of shallow waters
- Usually occurs in fast or moderate flowing waters. It appears unable to withstand the effects of siltation as its close relative, the goldeye, can
- Spawns in the spring when large numbers ascend rivers and small streams

The mooneye is restricted to the far mid-western corner of our range. For this reason it is of almost no importance to anglers or commercial fishermen within this region. Even to the west, where the mooneye is more common, it is not often actively sought. Commercial fishermen include a fair number of the closely related goldeye in their catch. Some of this number may, in fact, be mooneye.

The mooneye is included here to reduce the risk of its being confused with other fishes which it resembles.

Catfishes

Channel Catfish

Ictalurus punctatus

Local Names:

- Channel Cat
- Great Lakes Catfish
- Spotted Catfish
- Lake Catfish
- Barbue de Riviere

Distinguishing Characteristics:

- Deeply forked caudal fin distinguishes it from all other catfishes in our range
- Barbels on snout, lower lip, and the terminal end of the maxillary
- Usually a few spots (generally darker than the ground) sprinkled over the body. These spots are absent in very small or very large fish

Average Size:

- 14-24 inches (36-61 cm.)
- 2-10 pounds (0.91-5 kg.)

Habits:

- Generally prefers cooler, clearer waters than do the rest of this tribe
- Occurs in large lakes, ponds and rivers
- Like all the catfishes, it is a bottom dweller and feeder

The channel catfish is the largest member of its family occurring within our range. It may also be the most popular of its nocturnal clan. Because of its preference for clear water, it is found in generally more attractive habitats than some other catfishes. It is primarily a bottom feeder, but will take a bait presented only a foot or two below the surface. *I. punctatus* is an active fish and will take artificial lures as well as natural baits. For artificials, it prefers small lead headed jigs allowed to drift with the current. Almost any bait, alive or dead, will attract the channel cat. Worms, minnows, cut meat, and cut fish take the largest numbers of these fish.

As a food fish the channel catfish is highly prized. Its flesh is firm, white, and flaky. It is very flavorful, and even considered too strong by some. Removal of the darker meat along the lateral line eliminates this problem. In the Great Lakes and St. Lawrence River, the channel catfish comprises a fair part of the commercial catch each year.

Yellow Bullhead
Ictalurus natalis

Local Names:

- Yellow Catfish
- Bullhead
- Yellow-belly Bullhead
- Barbotte Jaune

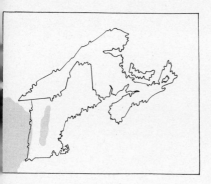

Distinguishing Characteristics:

- Caudal fin is distinctly rounded along its trailing edge
- Chin barbels are white or cream colored
- General body shape is more robust than in the brown bullhead

Average Size:

- 8-14 inches (21-36 cm.)
- ½-1 pound (0.22-0.45 kg.)

Habits:

- Prefers heavily weed-filled areas
- Usually found in the shallow waters of clear lakes, ponds, and slow moving streams
- Able to better withstand more adverse conditions than the other bullheads
- A nocturnal feeder, probing the bottom for a variety of food

It is unlikely that most fishermen are even aware of the presence of this fish within our region. Only a few anglers seek either of our native bullheads. Probably even fewer still make a distinction between the two species. Since both species move about in loose groups and are willing to take almost any bait, they are usually taken by youngsters or other anglers while bait fishing for other species.

Still fishing (from shore or a boat) with bait held just above the bottom by means of a float is the method most commonly used to take these bottom feeders.

The sharp spine on the leading edge of the dorsal fin may inflict painful wounds. Care must be taken to avoid such injury while removing bullheads from the hook.

Brown Bullhead

Ictalurus nebulosus

Local Names:

- Marbled Bullhead
- Brown Catfish
- Hornpout
- Catfish
- Mudcat
- Barbotte Brune

Distinguishing Characteristics:

- Rear margin of caudal fin has a distinctly squared shape
- Usually less deep than yellow bullhead
- Chin barbels are black or dark brown
- Adipose fin is long

Average Size:

- 6-12 inches (15.24-31 cm.)
- ¼-1 pound (0.11-0.45 kg.)

Habits:

- Occurs in quiet, usually mud bottomed lakes, ponds, and slow moving streams
- Is a nocturnal feeder but can be taken by anglers at any time of day
- Both our native bullheads exhibit an interesting behavior pattern around the hatching of the fry. When the eggs hatch, the very dark colored young form a dense school which is jealously guarded by the male parent for several weeks

Glossary

_____

A.

adipose fin
    a small fleshy fin-like projection found behind the dorsal fin on Salmonid and a few other fish families

amidship
    the mid section of a boat or other watercraft

amphipod
    small aquatic crustaceans which comprise a large portion of the diets of small and immature fishes

anadromous
    referring to those fishes which are born in fresh water, spend a majority of their mature lives in salt water, and return to fresh water to spawn

anal fin
    the fin, found on the median line of a fish's belly, immediately behind the vent

angler
    one who fishes with a hook, now refers to any sports fisherman

B.

bait

anything used to lure fishes — usually refers to living or dead organic matter used to attract fishes to a hook

bait fish

any small fish which is consumed by game species

bag (limit)

the maximum number of fish which may be legally taken from any body of water

barbel

slender, thread-like projections found on the heads of some fishes and serving as sensory organs, usually for the detection of food

barbs

found on fish hooks and harpoons, are sharp protrusions pointing in a direction opposite to that of the main hook's point and designed to prevent the main point from slipping out of a fish

basking

occurs when a fish lies very near the surface of the water, usually exposing its dorsal and caudal fins

bill fish

any species of fish having its upper jaws taper to a long spear-like projection. Usually refers to sailfish or marlin

block and tackle

a set of ropes and pullies rigged on a stout pole used to hoist large fish onto a boat, used in big-game salt water fishing

bog

a shallow, often weedy, body of water usually formed by the damming of a slow marsh stream

butterfly dressed

a method of preparing fish by cutting down the back, removing the head and spreading the body out — often used for drying or smoking

272

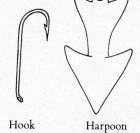

Barbs

Hook   Harpoon

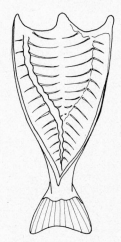

Butterfly dressed

C.

catadromous
> referring to those fishes which are born in salt water, live in fresh water for most of their lives, and return to salt water to spawn

caudal fin
> the tail or tail fin in fishes

caudal peduncle
> that area of the fish between the anal and caudal fins

caviar
> the eggs of the sturgeons prepared in salt and used as an appetizer

chum
> finely ground fish or other organic matter which is scooped into the water around a fisherman's boat to attract game fishes, usually in salt water

chum slick
> that fairly narrow band of water in which the chum tends to drift away from the fisherman's boat

Continental Shelf
> a relatively shallow submarine plain which extends outward from the coast and ends in a steep drop to much deeper water

copepod
> one of a large sub-class of fresh and salt water crustaceans which are consumed in great quantity by small fish and other animals. They are at a very low level on the food chain

corselet
> leathery or hard skin found on some fishes' bodies — usually occurs just behind the head

cosmopolitan
> refers to fishes which have oceanic or world-wide distribution

crustacean

    any member of a large class of fresh water and marine invertebrates which include crabs and lobsters

cut bait

    any bait, usually fish, which has been cut into small pieces

D.

dart

    the pointed forward end of a harpoon which pierces the fish

dorsal

    the back or upper part of a fish's body

dorsal fin(s)

    those fins found on the fish's back

dry fly

    an artificial fly designed to float on the surface of the water and imitate a living insect; most commonly used in trout and salmon fishing

drying (fish)

    the process wherein fish (i.e., cod) are salted and air dried to preserve the meat

Dry fly

E.

estuary

    a body of water in which salt water combines with the outflow of freshwater rivers. Estuaries are, for marine organisms, one of the most important breeding grounds and nurseries

F.

feather lure

    a lure which is made by tying long feathers or hairs to the rear of a metal head so that the hook is concealed by the feathers; most often used for tuna or other "big game" species

finlets

    very small fins (usually arranged in rows) on the dorsal and ventral median lines of certain species of fish (esp. the mackerels and tunas)

Feather lure

274

fish culture
procedures developed for the artificial propagation of fish

fish trap
a device (usually made of a net material) which is permanently set in an area of water for the purpose of catching food fishes

flank
the lower portions of the sides of a fish

flat (salt water)
a large area of sand or weed beds, close to shore which is covered by shallow water

float
any small piece of buoyant material used to keep the fisherman's hook or net suspended at a certain depth of water, also called a bobber

flowage
a body of slow moving water connecting two (usually larger) bodies of water; beaver ponds are often referred to as flowage

fly-fishing
a method of fishing which uses imitations of a fish's natural food (usually made from fur, feathers and other light weight materials) secured to the hook as a lure

fly line
a large diameter, relatively heavy line which carries the much lighter fly to the desired water

fly reel
a simple open spool type reel which holds the line in fly fishing

fly rod
a long fishing rod used in fly fishing

food chain
a succession of organisms in which the next lowest member is used as a food source

forage fish
small fish which serve as food for larger predators

Fly reel

Fly rod

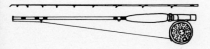

freestone stream
   a stream whose bottom is usually composed of granite or other loose rock; generally having acid water

fry
   young fishes just recently hatched

G.

gaff
   a large barbless metal hook used to lift game fishes from the water

gin pole
   a stout pole set on the deck of a fishing boat and used to haul heavy fish aboard

glide
   a portion of a stream or river where the water moves rapidly but remains unbroken

ground fish
   any salt water fish which spends most of its life near the ocean floor

guide
   a person employed by sport fishermen to aid them in finding and catching fish

guide (on fishing rods)
   circular metal or ceramic frames attached to a fishing rod at regular intervals which hold the line close to the rod

Gulf Stream
   the warm Atlantic Ocean current which originates in the Gulf of Mexico and flows north along the Atlantic coast

H.

habitat
   that environment in which a fish is most commonly found

haloed
   those spots found on fishes which are surrounded by a lighter circle of color

harpoon
 a long pole with a sharp point attached to a rope which is used to spear large game fishes

homogenized
 a condition which occurs in deep cold lakes in the Spring when sun and wind act on the water to make the temperature uniform throughout

hybrid
 a species of fish which results from the cross-breeding of two separate or distinct parent species

I.

ice-fishing
 a method of fishing wherein holes are drilled or chopped through the frozen surface of the water and a bait or lure is lowered through the hole to entice fish to strike

ice out
 that brief period (usually about two weeks) occurring just after the ice has melted from lakes and ponds in the Spring of the year

ice shanties
 small shelters built to protect ice-fishermen from the elements

inferior mouth
 any fish's mouth which is situated on the underside of the head such as in suckers

in-shore
 that loosely defined area of salt water which is relatively close to shore

inter-tidal zone
 that portion of the marine environment which is directly effected by the daily movement of the tides

invertebrate
 any animal which lacks a backbone

Inferior mouth

277

jig (lead headed)
   a fishing lure made by attaching hair or feathers to the rear portion of a molded lead weight containing a hook; designed to be fished by jerking the line upward and then allowing the lure to sink back before repeating

L.

landlocked
   any population of fish which has no access to the sea

lateral line
   that line along the sides of fishes made up of minute tubes containing mucus and serving as a sensory organ

leader
   that segment of the fishing line which connects the main portion of the line to the hook, usually made of monofilament or steel

leading edge
   the forward portion of a fish's fins

limestone stream
   a river or stream which flows over a limestone bed; these streams have a high alkaline content and house a great number of aquatic insects and crustaceans

lobes
   the upper and lower portions of a fish's tail fin taken separately

Lobster boat

lobster boat
   a small semi-open ocean going fishing boat designed for work in lobstering and often converted for tuna fishing

lunate
   when referring to a fish, means a crescent shaped fin

lure
   any artificial device used to attract and hook fish

May fly

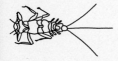

Nymph

M.

margin
    any of the edges of a fish's anatomy (i.e. fins, eyes, etc.)

maxillary
    the upper jaw of any fish

May fly
    an aquatic insect which constitutes a large part of the diet of fresh water fishes especially trouts and salmons

migration
    the movements of fishes usually for spawning or feeding purposes

mollusk
    any of a large group (phylum) of invertebrate animals (which includes snails, shellfish, etc.)

N.

native
    those fishes which spawn within a given area

night crawler
    a large earthworm which can be found on the surface of grassy areas (such as lawns) after dark; commonly used as bait for game fishes

nymph
    one of the immature stages in the development of aquatic insects

O.

off-shore
    fishing areas which lie far at sea, away from the shore

opercule
    a fish's gill covers, that hard, bony structure which covers the gill-rakers

P.

pan fish
　　any small fish, especially of the sunfish and perch family

party boat (or head boat)
　　a boat used for carrying fee paying customers on a fishing trip (usually in salt water)

pectoral fin(s)
　　the first or uppermost of the paired fins

pelagic
　　those fishes which spend most or all of their lives in the open sea

planting (stocking)
　　the introduction of hatchery reared fish to a body of water

plug
　　an artificial lure usually designed to imitate a bait fish

Plug

pool (in a river or stream)
　　that portion of the river or stream where its bed generally flattens and deepens causing the moving water to slow considerably; this is usually the most suitable area for the game fishes inhabiting that water

popper
　　a lightweight artificial lure designed to skip across the surface of the water, making a popping sound

Popper

R.

ray(s)
　　the small cartilaginous rods which give support to the soft fins of fishes

reel
　　a revolving or stationary spool attached to the butt end of a fishing rod, used for storing the line

restoration
　　the re-establishment of any species of fish which has been severely depleted

280

roe
> the eggs of fishes

rooting
> that feeding behavior in which fishes probe a muddy or other soft bottom for food

S.

scales
> small, hard plates which form the external covering of fishes

school
> a large group of fishes which travels together, usually comprised of one species

schute
> a hard bony plate found on the skin of certain fishes especially sturgeons and jacks

Sea lamprey
> an eel-like non-bony fish whose mouth is full of small rasp like teeth with which it attaches itself to the body of larger fishes and feeds on their fluids

seining
> a method of commercial fishing in which a net is drawn around a school of fishes, the net is then closed and hauled aboard the fishing vessel

selectivity
> occurs when game fishes begin feeding exclusively on one type of food

sewn on bait
> a live bait which is usually hooked in more than one place

shoal
> a submerged ledge around which fish often gather

shoal
> a school of fish

shoal
> an area of shallow water

Sewn on bait

skipping bug
a large fly-rod lure designed to make a popping or gurgling sound when moved across the surface of the water

smoking
a method of curing fish in which the flesh is hung over a bed of slowly burning wood chips

spawning
the reproductive act of fishes in which the female deposits the eggs after which the male covers them with sperm or "milt"

spawning bed
that area of bottom on which certain species of fishes deposit their eggs, often a depression made by the female

species
a division in animal classification which groups individuals having similar form and attributes

spine
a usually hard bone-like rod which supports the fins of certain fishes

Spinner

spinner
a piece of metal attached to a fishing line which revolves when drawn through the water

spinning
a method of sport fishing in which a reel with a fixed spool is attached to the rod so that it hangs below. A relatively heavy lure (or other weight) pulls a light line when the cast is made

Spinning rod and reel

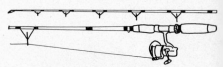

spring hole
a small area in a body of fresh water where a spring enters

stand
a sturdy plank attached to the bow of a tuna boat in which the harpooner stands

still fishing
a method of fishing in which a bait or lure is dropped into the water from a non-moving boat or pier

Stone fly

Streamer fly

Terminal mouth

stonefly
    an aquatic insect having two pairs of wings of nearly equal size, a favorite food of trouts and salmons

straggler
    a fish or group of fish which has strayed beyond its usual range

stray
    (see straggler)

streamer fly
    a fishing lure made of feather or hair which is designed to imitate a bait fish

subspecies
    a localized population of fish which differs slightly from the main species

swim bladder
    the bladder in fishes which remains filled with air and maintains the fish's stability in the water

swimming plug
    a fishing lure which is made to dive deep into the water and move with a wiggling motion when drawn along by the fisherman

T.

tail walking
    occurs when a game fish makes a leap in which it remains out of the water for a prolonged period by moving its caudal fin rapidly from side to side

tagging
    marking fish for future study by attaching a metal or plastic tag or clipping any one of the fins

temperate
    water of a moderate temperature

terminal mouth
    a fish's mouth which is located at the point of the head

thoroughfare
    a waterway connecting larger bodies of water

tidal rip
 an area of rough turbulent water created by the movement of the tides

tippet
 the small terminal end of a leader attached to the fly

tournament tackle
 fishing equipment which is designed and classified for the purpose of taking game fish of record size

tower
 a high platform added to the top of a boat used to sight game fishes

trailing edge
 the rear margin of any part of a fish's anatomy

trolling
 a fishing method which requires the use of a boat from which lines and bait or lures are moved through the water

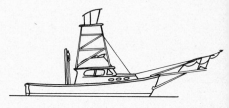

Tower

Stand (or Pulpit)

U.

ultra-light
 any very light weight fishing equipment

V.

ventral
 pertaining to the abdomen

voracious
 any fish which has a seemingly insatiable appetite i.e., bluefish, pikes, sharks, etc.

W.

watershed
 any bodies of water, lakes, streams, rivers and ponds which are interconnected and flow into a communal system

Weedless lure

weed bed
    a shallow area in a lake, pond, or river which is filled with aquatic vegetation

weedless lure
    a fishing lure designed to be used in weeds without hooking them

wet fly
    any fly which is designed to be fished under water

winch
    a drum or flange which is driven by hand or a motor and designed to haul heavy loads

Bibliography

Bigelow, Henry B. and	*Fishes of the Gulf of Maine*
Schroeder, William C.	United States Fish and Wildlife Service
Washington	1953
Burton, Robert and Maurice	*Encyclopedia of Fish*
London	Octopus Books Ltd.
	1975
Everhart, W. Harry	*Fishes of Maine* 2nd. Ed.
Augusta	The Maine Department of Inland Fisheries and Game
	1958
Freeman, Bruce L. and Walford	*Angler's Guide to the United States Atlantic Coast*
Seattle	Sections I, II, and III
	National Marine Fisheries Service
	1974
Jordan, David Starr and	*American Food and Game Fishes*
Everman, Barton Warren	Dover Publications
New York	1969
LaMonte, Francesca	*North American Game Fishes*
New York	Doubleday & Co., Inc.
	1945

LaMonte, Francesca
  New York

Marine Game Fishes of the World
Doubleday & Co., Inc.
1952

Leim, A. H. and Scott, W. B.
  Ottawa

Fishes of the Atlantic Coast of Canada
Fisheries Research Board of Canada
1966

McAllister, D. E. and Crossman,
  E.J.
  Ottawa

A Guide to the Freshwater Sport Fishes of Canada
National Museums of Canada
1973

Migdalski, Edward C.
  New York

The Fresh and Salt Water Fishes of the World
Alfred A. Knopf, Inc.
1976

Reece, Maynard
  New York

Fish and Fishing
Meredith Press
1963

Scarola, John F.
  Concord

Freshwater Fishes of New Hampshire
New Hampshire Fish and Game Department
Division of Inland and Marine Fisheries
1973

Scott, W. B.
  Toronto

Freshwater Fishes of Eastern Canada
University of Toronto Press
1954

Scott, W. B. and Crossman, E. J.
  Ottawa

Freshwater Fishes of Canada
Fisheries Research Board of Canada
1973

Tryckare, Tre and Cagner, E.
  New York

The Lore of Sportfishing
Crown Publishers
1976

Waterman, Charles F.
  New York

The Fisherman's World
Random House

Zim, Herbert S. and Shoemaker,
  Hurst H.
  New York

Fishes
Simon and Schuster
1956

Various Authors
Washington

Book of Fishes
National Geographic Society
1952

Index to Common Names

Index to Scientific Names